How to Overcome Any Challenge in Life
Through the Word Of God

VICTORY
IN
TROUBLED
TIMES

MATTHEW ALLARIA

26 25 24 23 22   8 7 6 5 4 3 2 1

VICTORY IN TROUBLED TIMES
Copyright ©2022 Matthew Allaria

Published by:
Emerge Publishing, LLC
9521 B Riverside Parkway, Suite 243
Tulsa, OK 74137
www.emerge.pub

Library of Congress Cataloging-in-Publication Data:
ISBN: 978-1954966-17-8 Perfect Bound
E-book available exclusively on Kindle

Printed in the United States

TABLE OF CONTENTS

CHAPTER 1

GOD'S WILL IS VICTORY

D id you know that victory is the will of God for your life? God does not want us to be overtaken by the enemy or anything the enemy throws at us. God does not want us to live defeated lives. He does not want us to live under the thumb of anxiety and depression. God does not want us to live under the oppressive hand of sickness and disease. God does not want us to live bound by the power of sin and addiction. God wants us to triumph, to overcome and to experience victory in every area of our lives.

God created us to be overcomers. 1 John 5:4 says, "For whatsoever is born of God overcomes the world: and this is the victory that overcomes the world, even our faith." The question you must answer is, "Are you born of God?" It is an easy question to answer. 1 John 5:1 says, "Whosoever believes that Jesus is the Christ is born of God." If you believe that Jesus is the Christ, then you are born of God. Now friend, verse 4 says, "Whatsoever is born of God overcomes the world." That tells me that if I am born of God, then

I was born to win. I was created for victory. I was not created to live a defeated existence. I was not created to be defeated by the devil or anything he tries to throw at me. If you are born of God, then neither were you! As believers, we are to be a victorious people. We are to be a people who enjoy victory in this life over our adversary!

I'VE NEVER LIKED LOSING

Early in my walk with the Lord, it was a thrilling thing for me to discover that God wanted me to live in victory. I played sports for most of my life, and as far back as I can remember, I have never liked losing. I played tee ball when I was five years old, and I didn't like losing then. I played sports against my older brother growing up, and I didn't like losing to him. As a young boy, I would sometimes cry if I lost or even if the team I was rooting for lost. As a little boy, I was a fan of the Saint Louis Cardinals, and I cried when they lost. Our local high school baseball team lost in the state championship game once, and as a little boy that made me cry. When I tell you that I have never liked losing, I mean what I say. I mean, let's get real, who likes to lose? Herman Edwards, a well-known football coach, once famously said in a press conference, "You play to win the game!" Nobody plays a game wanting to lose. You play to win the game! You want to defeat your opponent and enjoy the thrill of victory. Now, losing a baseball game as a young boy does not mean that much. Your favorite sports team losing a game also does not mean a whole lot in the grand scheme of things. However, God's people being defeated by the devil and missing the plan of God for their lives? That is a big deal.

As believers, we should not accept defeat when it comes to the enemy and what he's trying to do in our lives. We need to have the look of victory in our eyes and the cry of victory in our hearts. In 2 Corinthians 4:8, the Apostle Paul wrote, "We are troubled on every side, yet not distressed; we are perplexed, but not in despair; persecuted, but not forsaken; cast down, but not destroyed." He is saying, "Things might not look good right now, but we are winning this thing." This has to be the cry of our hearts, no matter what we are facing and no matter what is going on in our lives. It may not look good, all hell might be breaking loose and defeat might seem inevitable, but in the midst of all that, you have to declare, "I'm coming through this! I'm coming over this! I won't be defeated by this! God created me to be a winner and I will experience victory in this situation!"

VICTORY IS A BLESSING AND GOD WANTS YOU BLESSED

God makes it very clear to us in His Word that His will for His people is to live in victory. Deuteronomy 28 lists the blessings that were to come on God's people when they obeyed Him. Starting in verse 7, God reveals to us that victory is part of that blessing. Verse 7 says, "The Lord shall cause your enemies that rise up against you to be smitten before your face: they shall come out against you one way and flee before you seven ways." Now, an enemy is something or someone that/who is against you. An enemy is something or someone that/who is against your prosperity. Sickness and disease are enemies. Depression and anxiety are enemies. Strife in your family or in your marriage is an enemy. Lack of provision is an enemy. These are things that rise up against your well-being. All these things, of course, are the work of the devil. God wants every enemy that rises up against His people to be defeated. Isaiah 54:17 says, "No weapon that is formed against you shall prosper." This was a promise God was making to His people. You can see very clearly from these verses that God does not want His people to live in defeat. In Deuteronomy 28:13 this theme of victory continues. Verse 13 says, "And the Lord shall make you the head and not the tail; and you shall be above only and you shall not be beneath." You won't be on the bottom and be overcome by your adversaries, but are going to live in victory and be on the top instead.

The opposite of being blessed and enjoying victory over your enemies is to be cursed and to live in defeat. In the latter part of Deuteronomy 28 it begins to list the curse that would come on God's people if they didn't obey God's voice. Deuteronomy 28:15 says, "It shall come to pass, if you will not hearken unto the voice of the Lord your God, to observe to do all his commandments and his statutes which I command you this day; that all these curses will come upon you and overtake you." Then God reveals that being defeated by your enemies is a cursed existence. Verse 25 says, "The Lord shall cause you to be smitten before your enemies." This is part of a cursed existence, and God does not want this for His people. God does not want that for you. Verse 48 says, "You shall serve your enemies which the Lord shall send against you, in hunger, and in the thirst, and in nakedness, and in want of all things; and he shall put a yoke of iron upon your neck, until he has destroyed you."

Serving your enemies and being destroyed is a cursed existence. God does not want His people cursed and defeated. God wants His people blessed and enjoying victory!

VICTORY ALL OF THE TIME

God wants His people to walk in victory all of the time. 2 Corinthians 2:14 says, "Now thanks be unto God, which always causes us to triumph in Christ." If God always causes us to triumph, that means there is never a time that we experience defeat. If God always causes us to triumph, that means we overcome everything that comes against us. This scripture paints a picture of victory all of the time and victory over everything. In fact, say this out loud, "I experience victory all the time and I experience victory over everything." Be encouraged today, Friend, that victory belongs to you, and the victorious life is the kind of life that you are supposed to be living. Victory over addiction belongs to you. Victory over anxiety and depression belongs to you. Victory over family issues belongs to you. Victory over sickness and disease belongs to you.

GO YANKEES!

I have been a sports fan my whole life. I mentioned earlier how I was a big Saint Louis Cardinals fan; I was also a very big Ozzie Smith fan. In fact, I got to meet Ozzie Smith during my youth, and he signed my baseball glove. I had a small baseball glove with his signature already stamped on the glove, and before he autographed it, he saw the stamped signature on the inside and put that little glove on his big hand and smiled and said, "This is a nice glove." I was all about the Saint Louis Cardinals and all about Ozzie Smith. However, in the late 1990s a great change took place in my life. The Saint Louis Cardinals were consistently making it to the playoffs but kept failing to win the World Series. One year, in fact, the Cardinals were up 3 games to 1 in a best-of-7 series against the Atlanta Braves, with the winner moving on to the World Series, and the Cardinals blew it. That pushed me over the edge. I was tired of losing. About that time, the New York Yankees started to win a bunch of World Series championships, often in dramatic fashion, and that led me to becoming a New York Yankees fan. I even converted my younger brother to a New York Yankees fan so that he wouldn't have to endure the heartache of losing. Over the years, people have given me a hard time about being a Yankees fan because the Yankees are a very polarizing baseball team. I always tell people I like winning, and I root for greatness. I was tired of being on the losing side.

As believers, we never have to be on the losing side of any battle. Through faith in God, and with the help of the Holy Spirit, we can experience victory all the time, every time, over everything that comes against us.

DECISIVE VICTORIES

Romans 8:35–37 says, "Who shall separate us from the love of Christ? Shall tribulations, or distress, or persecution, or famine, or nakedness, or peril, or sword? Nay in all these things we are more than conquerors through him that loved us." As believers, God created us to be more than conquerors. This phrase, "more than conquerors," means to gain a decisive victory. God not only wants us to win, but He wants us to win in a decisive fashion!

I was fortunate enough to play on some very good high school sports teams in my high school days. I was the starting quarterback on a very good football team both my junior and senior year of high school. I was on a team with some very talented players, and we had some very good coaches. During my high school football career, we finished the regular season 9-0 both seasons that I started at quarterback. We enjoyed some very decisive victories both of those years. We won multiple games by more than four touchdowns. These were decisive victories. However, my junior year we experienced a decisive defeat in the first round of the playoffs, losing 42-21. I have been on a team that enjoyed a decisive victory and I've been on a team that experienced a decisive defeat, and I can tell you decisive victory is better. When the Apostle Paul wrote by the Spirit of God, "We are more than conquerors," God was revealing to us that He wants us to enjoy decisive victory in our lives.

Kenneth Hagin Sr. began a worldwide ministry in the 1930s and expanded it all the way to the turn of the century. The Lord used his ministry to bless many people all over the world. Two of the main things he ministered on was faith and healing. Kenneth Hagin was born with a deformed heart and an incurable blood disease. The doctors did not expect him to live long. At the age of 15, he became paralyzed and bedridden. One day while reading his Bible, he read Mark 11:22-24 and discovered that he could be supernaturally healed. Later, he was in fact supernaturally healed from his deformed heart and incurable blood disease. Then, for the next 60 years, he preached faith and healing and helped others to get healed and enjoy victory over the enemy. That is a decisive victory over the devil! The devil tried to kill him with sickness and disease, and not only did he receive his healing and get victory over the enemy, he helped others do it as well! That is making the devil wish he never would have attacked Kenneth Hagin. Kenneth Hagin made the devil eat it! Friend, you can have the same testimony. Whatever the devil is attacking you with, you can have a decisive victory over him. You can win, not by an inch, not by a foot, but by a mile! You can enjoy a landslide victory! You can make the devil eat it and wish he never would have attacked you to begin with! You are more than a conqueror!

DOES LIVING BY FAITH MEAN YOU'LL NEVER HAVE ANY CHALLENGES?

Just because God's will for our lives is victory does not mean that we will never experience any adversity. A lot of people hear teaching like this and say, "You are just telling people that if they have faith they will never have any problems." That is false on both accounts. That is not what I'm saying, and living by faith does not exempt you from experiencing challenges and attacks in your life. In John 16:33, Jesus said, "In the world you shall have tribulation." Tribulation means pressure, trouble and distress. Psalm 34:19 says, "Many are the afflictions of the righteous." Affliction means distress and adversity. All through the Bible we see men and women of faith coming under attack and experiencing adversity.

Why do we experience adversity in this life? It all has to do with the environment in which we live; Earth is a very hostile place.

We have an adversary who roams Earth every day looking to steal, kill and destroy. This is the first reason that we experience adversity, attacks and trouble in this life. In John 10:10, Jesus said, "The thief comes not, but for to steal, and to kill, and to destroy." Satan wants to steal, kill and destroy in every person's life, — including yours and mine. The enemy is behind all the chaos, turmoil and disaster happening in the world. 1 Peter 5:8 says, "Be sober, be vigilant; because your adversary the devil, as a roaring lion, walks about, seeking whom he may devour." You can see right there in that verse that you have an adversary. You have an enemy who is against you. He doesn't want things to go well for you in your life. He is walking the Earth, and he is looking to devour everything and everyone that he possibly can.

The second reason that we experience adversity in this life is because the curse is running rampant on Earth. This too makes Earth a very hostile place. The curse is everything bad that came to Earth when Adam sinned. Isaiah 24:6 says, "Therefore hath the curse devoured the earth." You see, Friend, the curse devours. The curse devours minds, bodies, families, provision and everything else. The curse includes things like sickness, poverty, anxiety, depression and strife. The curse that operates on Earth makes our planet a very dangerous place.

In this life there are things to overcome. Earth is not a harm-free, danger-free, enemy-free environment. This is why we experience things like pressure and adversity. Heaven is a harm-free, danger-free, enemy-free environment. The enemy is not in Heaven. The curse is not in Heaven. As a result, in Heaven you will experience no adversity, no attacks and no trouble. If you removed the enemy and the curse from this Earth, it would no longer be a hostile place. If you removed the enemy and the curse from this Earth, we would never experience any adversity, challenges or attacks. We do not live in that kind of environment yet. We live in a curse-filled, death-laden, enemy-present environment. Earth is a hot zone. Our existence on Earth is similar to that of a solider living in the United States who is called to active duty in a military hot zone. The United States of America is not a hot zone compared to the place he is going. The place he is going is littered with trouble that he will never experience in the United States. Well, similarly, this Earth is a hot zone. It is not without trouble, distress and adversity. Therefore, we should not be surprised when we experience an attack. 1 Peter 4:12 says, "Beloved, think it not strange concerning the fiery trial which is to try you, as though some strange thing happened unto you." Our enemy is here, the curse is here, and therefore we should not be shocked that we experience some adversity. The solider that is sent over to a hot zone is not surprised when he gets there and bullets are flying and people want to kill him. Nor should the believer be surprised that the enemy who is on this Earth wants to steal, kill and destroy. The adversity we experience has everything to do with the environment in which we live.

EXEMPT FROM DEFEAT, NOT ADVERSITY

As a believer, there are no scriptures that exempt you from trials, challenges and attacks. However, there are scores of scriptures that exempt you from being defeated by trial, challenge or attack. To preach "no challenges" is to preach contrary to the Word. Let me remind you: in John 16:33, Jesus said, "In the world you shall have tribulation." Psalm 34:19 says, "Many are the afflictions of the righteous." I am not telling you that you will never experience adversity or come under attack. Anyone who tells you that is not telling you the truth. Again, to preach "no challenges" is to preach contrary to the Word. However, to preach anything less than victory over every challenge is also to preach contrary to the Word. The mistake people make in quoting John 16:33 and Psalm 34:19 is they only quote half of the verse. John 16:33 says, "In the world you shall have tribulation: but be of good cheer; I have overcome the world." John 16:33 in The Amplified Bible says this, "I have told you these things, so that in Me you may have [perfect] peace and confidence. In the world you have tribulation and trials and distress and frustration; but be of good cheer [take courage; be confident, certain, undaunted]! For I have overcome the world [I have deprived it of power to harm you and have conquered it for you]." Jesus is telling us you will have challenges, but you can have victory over every one of them. Psalm 34:19 says, "Many are the afflictions of the righteous: but the Lord delivers him out of them all." If you are delivered out of them all, then you obtained victory over every one of them.

It is scripturally dishonest to only quote half of those verses and say, "Jesus said in the world we will have tribulation." Well, you only quoted half of the verse. It is disingenuous to say, "Many are the afflictions of the righteous." That's only half of the verse. You are highlighting the adversity and ignoring the victory.

You may be experiencing some adversity in your life right now. You may be right in the middle of a very trying time. It may feel like you are being attacked from every angle. You may be experiencing a great deal of pressure in your finances. You may be dealing with strong symptoms of anxiety and depression. You may be under attack in your physical body. However, as a believer you can experience victory over every attack. You can experience an abundance of God's provision and come out of that troubled time financially! You can be supernaturally delivered from anxiety and depression! You can be healed from every ailment in your body!

OUR VICTORY IS NOT JUST A HEAVENLY ONE

Many people believe John 16:33 and Psalm 34:19 are referring to the victory we enjoy once we get to Heaven. They believe the Lord delivers us from all of our afflictions when we leave this world and go to Heaven. That is a religious opinion and has no scriptural basis. I can prove that to you by looking at two verses. In 2 Timothy 3:11, the Apostle Paul wrote by the Spirit and said, "Persecutions, afflictions which came unto me at Antioch, at Iconium, at Lystra; what persecutions I endured: but out of them all the Lord delivered me." Friend, we ought to be smart enough to realize that Antioch, Iconium and Lystra are on Earth and not in Heaven. We ought to be smart enough to realize that Paul is writing this to Timothy when he is still on Earth and not when he was in Heaven. Therefore, he is saying I experienced pressure, afflictions and trouble on Earth — in Antioch, Iconium and Lystra — and the Lord delivered me out of them all. It was not a deliverance that Paul enjoyed when he got to Heaven, but one that he enjoyed on Earth. In 2 Timothy 4:17, the Apostle Paul wrote, "Notwithstanding the Lord stood with me, and strengthened me; that by me the preaching might be fully known, and that all the Gentiles might hear: and I was delivered from the mouth of the lion. And the Lord shall deliver me from every evil work, and will preserve me unto his heavenly Kingdom." The mouth of the lion that he was delivered from was not in Heaven. We do not have to wait to experience victory until we die and go to Heaven. We can experience victory over adversity right here and now on Earth. Our deliverance is not just a Heavenly deliverance. We do not just have to struggle through this life and wait to finally leave Earth to enjoy a Heavenly victory and deliverance. We can enjoy victory right now! Daniel was delivered from the lion's den on Earth. The three Hebrews were delivered from the fiery furnace on Earth. David got victory over Goliath on Earth. Our God is a God of victory! This Bible is a book of victory! God's people are to be a victorious people! You can experience victory over the things that are coming against you, and you do not have to wait till you get to Heaven to enjoy it!

VICTIM OR VICTOR?

The sad reality is that many people, Christians even, fight this idea of living in victory. They fight against the idea of God's people prospering, flourishing and doing well in this life. They fight for their right to struggle through this life. They fight for their right to be defeated in this life. There are a lot of people who get upset at people who preach victory in this life.

Many of those same people try to portray the Apostle Paul as someone who lived a defeated existence and preached a defeated gospel. They hear people preach victory and respond by saying, "Well, Paul had a lot of troubles." They try to portray the Apostle Paul as a man who lived this defeated and broken existence. Rather than take someone's word for how Paul lived and what he preached, let's let Paul speak for himself. In 2 Timothy 3:11, Paul wrote, "Persecutions, afflictions which came unto me at Antioch, at Iconium, at Lystra; what persecutions I endured: but out of them all the Lord delivered me." He is not saying he did not experience any trouble, but he is saying he experienced victory over all the trouble that came against him. Again, in 2 Timothy 4:17-18, he said, "Notwithstanding the Lord stood with me, and strengthened me; that by me the preaching might be fully known, and that all the Gentiles might hear: and I was delivered from the mouth of the lion. And the Lord shall deliver me from every evil work, and will preserve me unto his heavenly Kingdom." Being delivered from the mouth of the lion and being delivered from every evil work is not a defeated existence. In 2 Corinthians 4:8-9, he said, "We are troubled on every side, yet not distressed; we are perplexed, but not in despair; persecuted, but not forsaken; cast down, but not destroyed." There is no defeat in that language. Then in Philippians 4:11-13, writing from prison, he said,

Not that I speak in respect of want: for I have learned, in

whatsoever state I am, therewith to be content. I know both how to be abased, and I know how to abound: everywhere and in all things I am instructed both to be full and to be hungry, both to abound and to suffer need. I can do all things through Christ which strengthens me.

Before we try to portray Paul as some broken, defeated man who struggled through his whole life, we should let the man speak for himself. Even though he did experience adversity in his life, according to him, the Lord delivered him out of it all!

As Christians, we are not supposed to be a struggling, weak and defeated people. Rather, we are supposed to be a victorious bunch. The victories in our lives testify to the good God that we serve. When you experience victory over what is attacking you and people ask you how it happened, you can point them to your good God! Victories in our lives will actually draw others to the God we serve.

If you had to choose between two shepherds, I am certain you would look at the condition of the sheep to see what shepherd you would choose to follow. If you looked behind one shepherd and saw a bunch of sad, defeated and broken sheep, you would not choose to follow that shepherd. If you looked behind the other shepherd and you saw a bunch of joyful, peaceful and victorious sheep, you would choose to follow that one. Our victory is part of our testimony! When people see the goodness of God in our lives, it speaks of the Good Shepherd we follow. When we are enjoying victory over our adversary, it tends to draw those around us. It draws them to the good God we serve.

MY VICTORY IS NOT JUST FOR ME

Living a victorious life should be important to us because it is the only way that we can be a help to anyone else. God makes it clear in His Word that we are to be a blessing to other people. Acts 20:35 says, "I have showed you all things, how that so laboring you ought to support the weak, and to remember the Words of the Lord Jesus, how he said, 'It is more blessed to give than to receive.'" Romans 15:1 says, "We then that are strong ought to bear the infirmities of the weak." Galatians 6:2 says, "Be ye one another's burdens, and so fulfill the law of Christ." God told Abraham in Genesis 12:2, "I will bless you and make your name great; and you shalt be a blessing." We can see clearly from these verses that we are supposed to be a blessing and a help to other people. We are supposed to help others get to a place of victory. We cannot possibly do that if we live defeated lives.

In the 14th chapter of the book of Matthew, it records the account of Jesus and Peter walking on the water. Jesus was walking on the water and then Peter got out of the boat and began to walk on the water to go to Jesus. However, because Peter yielded to fear, he fell into the sea that night. He cried out for Jesus to save him, and Jesus stretched forth His hand and pulled Peter out of the water. As I read the account of that one day, the Lord asked me, "Do you know why Jesus was able to keep Peter from drowning?"

I said, "No Lord."

The Lord said to me, "Because Jesus wasn't drowning."

You have never seen a drowning man save another drowning

man. If you want to be able to keep someone from drowning, then you have to learn to walk on the water. If you are being defeated by life's challenges and obstacles, and are not walking in victory yourself, how will you help anybody else walk in victory? The answer is simple: You won't.

One of the great motivating factors for us to live in victory is that it positions us to be able to help others live in victory. The victory that you enjoy in your life is not just for you, but rather it positions you to be able to help someone else. If you have learned to yield to the Lord, trust Him and follow Him, and as a result you are enjoying victory in every area of your life, then you can help others get to that place as well. If you are bound by addiction yourself, how will you minister to someone else to help them get free? If you are being overtaken by anxiety and depression, you are not in a position to help someone else get free from those things. If your marriage is a mess, you won't be able to help someone else who is having marital problems. However, as we learn how to enjoy victory over these kinds of things, we are in a place where we can help others enjoy victory over these things as well.

One of the best examples of this is the Apostle Paul in the book of Philippians. The Apostle Paul wrote his letter to the Church of Philippi while he was in prison. He got thrown into prison wrongfully as he pursued the call of God on his life. He did not do anything wrong, but rather he was in prison because he was obeying God, following God and endeavoring to complete the assignment that God had put on his life. Now, many in this situation would go into the tank. Many would get depressed, feel sorry for themselves or even get mad at God, but not the Apostle Paul. In Philippians 4:11, he wrote,

I have learned, in whatsoever state I am, therewith to be content. I know both how to be abased, and I know how to abound: everywhere in all things I am instructed both to be full and to be hungry, both to abound and to suffer need. I can do all things through Christ which strengthens me.

Those are the Words of a man who is enjoying complete victory over the situation that he is facing. Those are not the Words of a sad and defeated man. Those are the Words of a victorious man. As a result of him being in a place of victory, he was able to continue to minister to others while he was in prison. By the unction of the Holy Spirit, he wrote the wonderful book of Philippians that ministered to the Church of Philippi then and is still ministering to us today. Had he been defeated, sad and depressed, he would not have been in a position to be used by the Lord to minister to other people. You can see that his own victory positioned him to be able to help others enjoy victory.

GOD CAN GET YOU OUT

My guess is that if you are reading this book, you quite possibly are facing a trying time right now in your life. It is my heart's desire to see you experience victory in that situation. I want to see God move on your behalf and completely deliver you from whatever is attacking you.

To experience victory in troubled times there is a truth that you must lay hold of, and it is this: God can get you out. You may be facing a lot of trouble right now. You may be under a great deal of pressure. The pressure you are facing may be heavier than any pressure you've experienced before. You may have found yourself right in the middle of a very trying time. Friend, in spite of that, God can get you out. No matter how great the pressure, no matter how big the problem, no matter how trying the time is, God can get you out.

You need to begin to stir your faith up to that reality. In fact, I want you to say this out loud, "God can get me out." Say it again, "God can get me out." One more time, "God can get me out." The enemy wants to throw you into a place of hopelessness where you begin to think there is no way out. He wants you to believe that your situation will never change. If you are going to enjoy victory, you have to fight against that hopelessness and begin to declare, "No Satan. Nothing is impossible for my God. Nothing is too hard for Him. He can get me out of this! He can bring me through this! He can cause me to overcome this!"

We serve a God who is famous for getting people out of hopeless situations. Psalm 40:1–3 says,

I wait patiently for the Lord; and He inclined unto me and heard my cry. He brought me up also out of the horrible pit, out of the miry clay, and set my feet on a rock, and established my goings. And he hath put a new song in my mouth, even praise unto God: many shall see it and fear, and shall trust in the Lord.

You can see in that verse that God brought David up out of a horrible pit. You may be in a horrible pit today, but it is not so horrible that God can't get you out. Psalm 113:7–8 says, "He raises the poor out of the dust, and lifts the needy out of the dunghill; that he may set him with princes." We serve a God that lifts people out of the dunghill and sets them with princes. Say this out loud again, "God can get me out. The God I serve is famous for giving people who are in hopeless situations great victories." Your situation may look hopeless. Maybe you have never been this low before. Maybe you have never seen darkness like this before. However, you need to remember the God you serve. His ability knows no bounds. In Genesis 18:14, He said, "Is there anything too hard for the Lord." Mark 10:27 says, "With God all things are possible." Our God has never encountered a problem that He could not solve. He has never met an enemy that He could not defeat. No person in the history of mankind has ever been in a situation so bad that God could not get them out of it. Say this out loud again, "God can get me out."

I WILL NOT, I WILL NOT, I WILL NOT

Our God is not a God who abandons His people when they are in trouble. Hebrews 13:5 (Amplified Bible) says, "For He [God] Himself has said, 'I will not in any way fail you nor give you up nor *leave you without support. [I will] not,* [I will] not, [I will] not in any degree leave you helpless nor *forsake* nor let [you] down (relax My hold on you)! [Assuredly not!].'" You have God's Word on it that He will not leave you. He will not abandon you in your time of need. God does not abandon us when we are under attack. In John 10:11, Jesus said, "I am the good shepherd… he that is a hireling and not the shepherd, whose own the sheep are not, sees the wolf coming and leaves the sheep, and flees. The hireling flees because he cares not for the sheep." It is the hireling that flees when his sheep are in trouble, but the Good Shepherd does not do that. When you are in trouble, God will jump in the trouble with you to get you out of the trouble. In Psalm 91:15–16, the Lord said, "He will call upon me, and I will answer him: I will be with him in trouble; I will deliver him, and honor him. With long life will I satisfy him, and show him my salvation." God does not abandon us when we are in trouble, but rather is with us and will deliver us. In Psalm 23:4, David wrote, "Though I walk through the valley of the shadow of death, I will fear no evil: for you are with me." God was with him in the valley of the shadow of death; He did not abandon him. In fact, Amos 3:12 paints a very graphic picture of the shepherd's commitment to his sheep. It says, "Thus saith the Lord, 'As the shepherd takes out of the mouth of the lion, two legs, or a piece of an ear; so shall the children of Israel be taken out that dwell in Samaria in the corner of a bed, and in Damascus in a couch.'" This reveals to us that a good shepherd will even go into the mouth of a lion to save one of his sheep. Jesus has already done that for us. He went into the mouth of the lion when He went into the pit of hell to save us from hell. This reveals to us that there is nothing our God wouldn't do to deliver us and put us in a place of victory.

THE WAY OUT

How are you going to enjoy victory in a troubled time? In John 14:6, Jesus said, "I am the way, the truth and the life." He is the way out of trouble and into victory. You are going to follow your Good Shepherd, for whom nothing is impossible, and He is going to lead you out of the trouble and into the place of victory. Let's read the 23rd psalm to discover where a good shepherd leads his sheep. It says,

The Lord is my shepherd; I shall not want. 2 He maketh me to lie down in green pastures: he leadeth me beside the still waters. 3 He restoreth my soul: he leadeth me in the paths of righteousness for his name's sake. 4 Yea, though I walk through the valley of the shadow of death, I will fear no evil: for thou art with me; thy rod and thy staff they comfort me. 5 Thou preparest a table before me in the presence of mine enemies: thou anointest my head with oil; my cup runneth over. 6 Surely goodness and mercy shall follow me all the days of my life: and I will dwell in the house of the Lord forever.

You will notice in this psalm that the Good Shepherd led the sheep through the valley of the shadow of death and into a place of victory!

LET'S BEGIN THE JOURNEY

Over the next five chapters we are going to go on a wonderful journey of learning how to experience victory in troubled times. In fact, I am going to give you five keys that I have learned from the Spirit of God that have propelled me to victory time and time again.

Back in 2012, I experienced an attack from the enemy like I never had before. I began to deal with a lot of fear and discouragement. Today, people would probably call it anxiety and depression. I was having negative thoughts and feelings in a way that I never had before. It just so happened that while I was experiencing these things, I was doing a series of teachings entitled, "No More Sad," where I was ministering on how to get victory over sorrow.

At that point in my life, I had been walking closely with the Lord for close to ten years, and I had been in ministry for close to nine of those years. I had preached faith and victory, and I had received a lot of revelation from the Lord on how to experience victory in my life, but I was finding it difficult to overcome this attack. One day, in a time of prayer, I was meditating on 1 John 5:4. It says, "For whatsoever is born of God overcomes the world; and this is the victory that overcomes the world, even our faith." While I was meditating on that verse, the Lord spoke to my heart and said, "Dance with the one that brung you." I could see at that moment that the Lord was reminding me that the principles of faith that He had taught me over the years had carried me through everything I had faced up until this point. I didn't need some new revelation to overcome the things I was facing, I needed to dance with the one who brung me. I needed to go back and apply the things that I knew to apply, because faith in God will always be our victory, and through faith in God we can overcome any attack that the enemy wages against us.

I think sometimes when we are under great pressure, we think we need some special revelation or some special word from God that we have never heard before. In our eyes, our problem is so big that the basic stuff we've learned won't be enough to help us overcome it. I have found that way of thinking to be completely false. What I've found is that in a time of pressure, usually what gets you over are the basic things you learned early on but have not been applying.

So often in the times of pressure, we don't need some special revelation. We need to go back and apply the basic principles of faith and the Word of God that we may have learned years ago. It is the application of the basics that will get you over and get you into a place of victory.

You notice I said the application of the basics? That is because knowing something and not doing it has never helped anybody. To see the power of the Word of God work in your life, you must practice it in your life.

In this book, I am going to give you five keys to experiencing victory in troubled times. These five keys are things the Lord revealed to me when I was under attack in my life. Anybody who wants to can apply these five principles in their life. They are not difficult to understand, but they do require some discipline to practice consistently. These five basic principles helped me to get into a place of victory, and I believe they will do the same thing for you!

CHAPTER 2

MAKE THE WORD OF GOD FINAL AUTHORITY

In a troubled time, it is absolutely vital that you make God's Word the final authority in your life. This is the first key to experiencing victory in troubled times. What does it mean to make the Word of God final authority? It means that we elevate God's Word above everything else and govern our lives based on what the Word of God says. We elevate the Word above what we see, above how we feel and even above the opinions of so-called experts. When the Word of God is the final authority in your life, you believe what the Word says, you say what the Word says and you act on what the Word says, and you do that in spite of what you see or how you feel.

THIS BIBLE IS GOD TALKING TO YOU

To make God's written Word the final authority in our lives, we first must acknowledge that all scripture is given by inspiration of God. 2 Timothy 3:16 says, "All scripture is given by inspiration of God, and is profitable for doctrine, for reproof, for correction, for instruction in righteousness: That the man of God may be perfect, thoroughly furnished unto all good works." From that verse, we can conclude that if it is in the Bible, then God is the one who inspired it to be written. The things contained in the Bible are not just one man writing a letter to another man. The Words in the Bible are not just one man writing a letter to a group of Christians thousands of years ago. No! These scriptures were penned at the inspiration of the Holy Spirit. God inspired that these things be written down for all men to have for all time.

God is infinite in wisdom, so one book certainly cannot contain all of His knowledge and wisdom. This reality makes the Bible even more precious because the things contained in it were hand selected by God and given to us. The things contained in those sixty-six books were hand selected by God. God could have inspired that a multitude of different things be written in the Bible, but the things that are in the Bible He personally hand selected for us. The things in the Bible are the things God wanted us to see, the things God wanted us to know, the things God wants us to have.

Think for a moment about having to select five things to write in a book and give to your children or grandchildren that would help them in their lives. Think about how selective you would be about those five things. You love your children and grandchildren so much, and as a result you would want to give them the things that would help them the most. You would thoughtfully and deliberately select those five things with great care. When you handed them that book, that book would be precious to you because the things in it are the things you chose to put in it to help them in their lives because you love them. This is a perfect picture of what God did in His written Word for us. In His love for us, and in His desire to see things go well for us, He hand selected that these things be placed in His Word.

The written Word of God is a gift that God has given to us. Let's look at 2 Timothy 3:16 again. It says, "All scripture is given by inspiration of God, and is profitable for doctrine, for reproof, for correction, for instruction in righteousness: That the man of God may be perfect, thoroughly furnished unto all good works." Look at that phrase, "All scripture is given..." As I read that one day, the Lord spoke to me and said, "Given to who, from whom?" Well, it was given to us and it is from God. It became a revelation to me that day that this Bible is a gift from God to me.

Many people foolishly try to downplay the contents of the Bible by saying, "Well that is God talking to the Jews. That is just Paul talking to Timothy. That is John writing a letter to Gaius." When people talk like this, they are endeavoring to downplay the significance of what is being said in scripture. In their belief, what is being said in the scripture is not God talking to them. The Bible is not just God talking to the Jews or Paul talking to Timothy or John talking to Gaius. The words in the Bible were given to me by God and therefore everything in this Bible is God talking to me. What do I mean? Well, in the scripture you are reading, God may be talking to Jews, but He inspired that it be written down for you, so God is saying something to you in that scripture. Paul may be talking to Timothy, but God is the one who inspired it to be written down for you, so God is saying something to you in that scripture. God's Word is God talking to you! God's Word is God talking to me!

If you are ever going to make the Word of God final authority in your life, then His Word has to be big to you. So many people do not make the Word of God final authority because to them it is just God talking to someone else, or it is just one man talking to another man. They do not see the written Word of God as being God-inspired. They do not see the written Word of God as God's gift to them. They do not see the written Word of God as God talking to them. As a result, they do not make His Word the final authority in their lives.

RAMBO - GET EQUIPPED

Why did God give us His Word in written form? What purpose does it serve in our lives? Let's read 2 Timothy 3:16 again. It says, "All scripture is given by inspiration of God, and is profitable for doctrine, for reproof, for correction, for instruction in righteousness: That the man of God may be perfect, thoroughly furnished unto all good works." That verse says God gave us His written Word so that we would be perfect and thoroughly furnished for all good works. The Word perfect in that verse means complete, fitted or prepared. The Word furnish means to equip fully. God gave us His written Word so that we would be perfected, completed, fitted, prepared and fully equipped. This is the purpose and function of God's Word in the life of a believer.

Now, growing up I loved Rambo. Rambo is a movie starring Sylvester Stallone that was made in the 1980s. I particularly liked Rambo II. In Rambo II, Rambo is going to Vietnam, and he was supposed to do some reconnaissance work and take pictures to find out if there were any prisoners of war there. Rambo, being Rambo, didn't just take pictures, but instead he ended up actually bringing a bunch of POWs home. Before Rambo leaves for his mission, he gets fully equipped. The dramatic and thunderous music begins, and Rambo is dressed in all black, and he is getting strapped with guns, grenades, knives and his all-important headband. I loved that part of the movie. In the military, before they send you on a mission, they equip you with what you need to be successful.

This is what the Word of God does for us. It equips us with what we need to enjoy victory over our enemy. As you and I spend time in the Word of God, it does this in our lives. The Word of God straps us up with everything we need to live victoriously in this life. If you are going to experience victory in troubled times, you need to be equipped to do so, and the Word of God is the very thing that will equip you. Therefore, in a troubled time, you must start with God's Word.

THE KEY TO SUCCESS

The Word of God is the foundation of our prosperity and success in this life. All throughout the Bible, when things did not go well for God's people, it was always a result of them ignoring God and ignoring His Word. God told Joshua in Joshua 1:8, "This book of the law shall not depart out of your mouth; but you shall meditate therein day and night, that you may observe to do according to all that is written therein: for then you shall make your way prosperous, and then you shall have good success." You see, God's Word is the foundation upon which our prosperity and success is built. Moses had just died after failing to lead God's people into the Promised Land. God is now calling Joshua to lead the people into the Promised Land. God is calling Joshua to do what Moses failed to do. This most likely was a very big endeavor in Joshua's eyes. Moses was the greatest man of God Joshua had ever seen. Moses led God's people out of Egyptian bondage. God used Moses to part the Red Sea. God used Moses to get water out of a rock. God used Moses to get bread rained down from Heaven. God is calling Joshua to do what the great Moses failed to do. Joshua is going to lead the people into the Promised Land. This is a big undertaking for Joshua. God is calling him to step into this position of leadership and lead God's people. It is clear from the scriptures in Joshua chapter 1 that Joshua was dealing with some fear in regards to this great endeavor. Three times, in a matter of four verses, God tells Joshua to be strong and courageous and to not be afraid. Then, in verse 8, God gives Joshua the key to success in this massive undertaking. Verse 8 again says, "This book of the law shall not depart out of your mouth; but you shall meditate therein day and night, that you may observe to do according to all that is written therein: for then you shall make your way prosperous, and then you shall have good success." God tells Joshua the key to success is His Word. He tells Joshua to meditate on the Word, day and night, keep it before you, keep it in your mouth, do what it says, and if you do, you will be prosperous and you will have good success.

If the Word of God was the key to Joshua's success in that massive undertaking, then it is the key to our success in troubled times. Many times, people will read verses in the Old Testament and think that does not apply to us because it is the Old Testament. This is not true. Romans 15:4 says, "For whatsoever things were written aforetime were written for our learning, that we through patience and comfort of the scriptures might have hope." These things in the Old Testament are written for our learning.

A reality that many people fail to acknowledge is that spiritual law does not change. Spiritual law is simply a principle laid out by God that says if you do this, then this will happen. Even though we have a new covenant, and even though we are no longer under the law of the old covenant, spiritual law works the same no matter what covenant you are under. When God said to Joshua, "This book of the law shall not depart out of your mouth; but you shall meditate therein day and night, that you may observe to do according to all that is written therein: for then you shall make your way prosperous, and then you shall have good success," that became spiritual law. That will work for us today just like it worked for Joshua all those years ago.

If we are going to experience victory in a troubled time, the Word of God will be at the center of our victory. The Word of God will be the foundation upon which our victory is built. You want to experience victory over anxiety and depression? You want to experience victory in the midst of a marital attack? You want to experience victory in the midst of a financial struggle? God just told you how in Joshua 1:8. In Matthew 4:4, when Jesus was being tempted by the devil, He said it like this: "Man shall not live by bread alone, but by every word that proceeds out of the mouth of God." That word live means to enjoy a blessed life. We live by the Word. We enjoy a blessed life by the Word. We experience victory in troubled times by the Word. If you and I are going to enjoy a blessed life and experience victory in times of trouble, the Word of God will be the root that produces that kind of fruit. Say this out loud, "I live by the Word! I win by the Word! I experience victory in troubled times by the Word!"

WHAT DOES THE WORD SAY?

To experience victory in troubled times, we have to run to the Word of God. Whatever challenge you are facing today, whatever trying situation you have found yourself in, whatever trouble you have encountered, there is a question you need to ask yourself, and it is a question that will change the course of your situation and even the course of your life. The question you have to ask yourself is, "What does God say about this in His Word?" What does God say in His Word about the challenge you are facing? What does God say in His Word about this situation? What does God say in His Word about the attack the enemy is waging against me? Why do we ask ourselves that question? Because the Word of God is the foundation to our success. The Word of God is the root that will produce the fruit of victory in our lives.

If you are struggling with anxiety and depression, you need to ask yourself, "What does God say about this in His Word?" If you are in the midst of a financial struggle, you need to ask yourself, "What does God say about this in His Word?" If you are experiencing symptoms of sickness and disease in your body, you need to ask yourself, "What does God say about this in His Word?" We have to train ourselves to run to the Word first.

A BABY THAT WON'T SLEEP

My wife Amber and I have two beautiful daughters named Grace and Faith. When Grace was around 10 months old, she still was not sleeping all the way through the night. Now, this was not a life-or-death situation, but it is good to practice spiritual principles in every area of your life and so we did. One of the first things we endeavor to do in situations like this is ask ourselves, "What does God say about this in His Word?" We did just that in this situation. Psalm 127:2 said, "He [God] gives his beloved sleep." We knew for a fact our sweet little baby Grace was God's beloved, and we knew He wanted to give her sleep. The Lord also led us to Proverbs 3:24: "Your sleep will be sweet." We started with the Word, we did what God told us to do, and we experienced a great victory in that situation. Grace went from not sleeping all the way through the night to sleeping all the way through the night for multiple months straight. (I'll share more about this story later in this book.)

To experience victory, we must start with the Word. When we find ourselves under attack or in challenging situations, it is absolutely vital that we ask ourselves the question, "What does God say about this in His Word." Why? Our prosperity and our success start with the Word of God.

A LONELY OLD PREACHER

I started with the Word of God when I was single and believing God for a spouse. At the time I was 25 years old, and I had been in ministry for close to four years, and I wanted a godly wife to go on this journey with me. I had been trained by mentors in the faith to go to the Word first and so I did. The Lord led me to multiple verses about having a wife. Proverbs 19:14 says, "A prudent wife is from the Lord." Proverbs 18:22 says, "Whoso finds a wife finds a good thing and obtains favor from the Lord." In Genesis, I saw that God gave Adam a wife. I knew Acts 10:34 said, "God is no respecter of persons." God showed me He was no respecter of persons. If He gave Adam a wife, He would give me a wife as well. I meditated in those scriptures about my wife often. At this time in my life, I was already preaching at my own services on Sunday mornings. As a result, I was not going to a church where I might be able to meet this godly woman who was to be my wife. I had graduated from college, so I was not around girls my age in that environment. I could go multiple days in a row and not even encounter a girl my age. I started thinking to myself, "How on earth am I even going to meet a woman to marry? Not to mention, a godly woman who loves the Word." Then the devil would jump in and say, "Yeah it is not going to happen buddy. You are not even around girls your age. Most of the girls you know who are around your age are not the godly woman that you are looking for. You are going to end up a lonely old preacher."

Remember, when you are having an experience like this, you need to ask yourself the question, "What does God say about this in

His Word?" I did that and the Lord led me to Genesis 2 when He was creating a wife for Adam. Verse 22 said, "And the rib, which the Lord God had taken from the man, made he a woman and brought her unto the man." Did you catch that last part? "Brought her unto the man." The Lord said to me, "You just go about your business pursuing me and pursuing my call on your life, and I will bring your wife to you." That verse absolutely set me free! I did not have to look for her; I did not have to find her because God told me through His Word and by His Spirit that He would bring her to me! On Thursday, May 17th, 2007, I had an evening service, so all day I was preparing to preach. I had no idea that the woman I was going to marry was coming to that service that night. My aunt had invited Amber's sister-in-law and Amber to come to the service. She came in the building; she sat down in a chair and listened to me preach. The Lord brought her to me just like He said He would in His Word! In our lives, we run to the Word and we start with the Word. We especially do this in the midst of a troubled time.

PASTORING IN A PANDEMIC

Three months into our first year of pastoring Northsmoke Church, the coronavirus hit the world. I was 38 years old and had been in ministry for over 16 years, but I had never pastored a church, and like most everybody else, I did not foresee a global pandemic hitting Earth when the church was three months old.

You may remember that when news of the coronavirus hit in mid-March of 2020, there was a lot of panic in the world, and unfortunately, in the Body of Christ. There were not only questions in regards to health and safety, but there were questions regarding how the coronavirus would affect the economy. Fear was running rampant and the gloom-and-doom birds were out.

Here we are leading a church for the first time, a global pandemic hits the earth, and fear seemingly was everywhere. What do we do? We run to the Word and we ask the question, "What does God say about this in His Word?" You see, our response does not change based on the gravity of the situation. We run to the Word first if we are trying to get a baby to sleep at night or if a global pandemic hits Earth. The Word always works! The Word will always produce victory, prosperity and success in the lives of people who will believe it and act upon it. Facing this situation that we never would have imagined in a million years, we ran to the Word. On Sunday, March 22nd, 2020, I preached a message entitled, "What Does the Word Say About Viruses and Plagues?" That Sunday we ministered to our congregation what God says about viruses and plagues in His Word. Our foundation text was Psalm 91. Psalm 91:3 says, "He shall deliver you from the noisome pestilence (plague)." Verses 5–7 say, "You shall not be afraid of for the terror by night; nor for the arrow that flies by day; Nor for the pestilence (plague) that walks in darkness; nor for the destruction that wastes at noonday. A thousand shall fall at your side, and ten thousand at your right hand; but it shall not come near you." Verse 10 says, "There shall no evil befall you, neither shall any plague come near your dwelling." You might be thinking, "Wasn't it hard to pastor during that time?" Honestly, because the Lord helped us, it was not hard. You just run to the Word and believe what the Word says. That is what we did and that is what we led our people to do. It was not but a week or so later that the gloom-and-doom birds were back, but this time it was about how the coronavirus would affect the economy. People were predicting recessions and depressions in the financial sector. What do you do? You run to the Word. What does God say in His Word about times of financial famine? We began to minister to our people out of the 37th psalm. Verses 18–19 say, "The Lord knows the days of the upright: and their inheritance shall be forever. They shall not be ashamed in the evil time: and in the days of famine they shall be satisfied." By the leading of the Spirit, we began to teach our people that we can have abundance even in a time of famine. Why did we teach that? Because that is what the Word says.

The enemy will always try to make things difficult in times of trouble, but things do not have to be difficult. Don't allow the enemy to make things difficult and bring confusion in your life. No matter what the situation is we run to the Word. We find out what the Word says. We believe what the Word says. We say what the Word says. We act on what the Word says. And that's it!

MISGUIDED PRAYER

Confused religion does not teach us to run to the Word. Confused religion teaches us to ask God repeatedly to do something about the situation we are facing. Many Christians that are in a troubled time have no idea what the Word says about their situation. They just beg God to do something for them. Many run to so-called "prayer," where they just beg God to do something for them, and they do not run to the Word. Now, let's be clear, there is nothing wrong with petitioning God in prayer, but that too needs to be done in line with the Word. In John 15:7, Jesus said, "If you abide in me, and my words abide in you, you shall ask what you will, and it shall be done unto you." According to Jesus, to have a fruitful prayer life, one of the prerequisites is that His Word must abide in you. The Word has to abide in you before you can pray effectively. There is no such thing as an effective prayer life apart from the Word of God. Many pray ineffectively because they pray without even knowing what the Word says. The Word is not abiding in them.

Why do so many love the idea of just running to God and asking Him to solve all their problems? Because this requires nothing of us. People love the idea of doing nothing and God doing everything based on their request. Having the Word abide in us, that takes effort on our part. So many do not want to put forth that effort. God did not tell Joshua, "Pay no attention to My Word, just ask Me for anything you need, and you will prosper and have good success." He told Joshua to meditate the Word, day and night. He told Joshua to not let the Word depart from his mouth. He told Joshua to do what My Word says and then you will prosper and have success. Many people do not like that because it requires something of them. Most like the idea of not doing any of that and just asking God to do something and having Him do it. However, that is not the way these things work.

Let me caution you about being in a troubled time and just begging God to do something for you without knowing what His Word says. Run to the Word first and ask God, "Lord, what do you have to say in Your Word about this thing that I am facing?"

Once you find out what the Word says, then you pray in line with the Word. You set your faith in agreement with those scriptures. Meditate in those scriptures that speak to your situation. You keep those scriptures concerning your situation in your mouth. This is prayer that is built upon the Word of God, and because it is, it actually works!

THE FINAL AUTHORITY

Once we have discovered what the Word says regarding our situation, the next thing we must do is make the Word of God final authority in our lives. That simply means that we decide to govern our lives, specifically with respect to the situation at hand, according to what the Word of God says. To make God's Word final authority means that you have decided to agree with the Word, believe the Word, think in line with the Word, talk in line with the Word and act like the Word of God is true in regards to your situation. For the Word of God to be final authority means that you align yourself with what the Word of God has to say in regards to your situation in every way possible.

You align with the Word in that manner because you have elevated the Word above everything else. This is another key element of making the Word of God final authority. You elevate the Word and what it says above everything else. You elevate the Word above what you see, above how you feel and even above the opinions of people or so-called experts. Psalm 138:2 (Common English Bible) says, "You have made your name and your word greater than everything else." This is at the heart of making God's Word final authority in your life. God's Word is greater than everything else. When my feelings contradict the Word, the Word is bigger than my feelings. When what I see contradicts the Word of God, the Word of God is bigger than what I see. When my own understanding contradicts the Word, the Word is bigger than my understanding. When the opinions of experts contradict the Word, the Word is bigger than the opinions of experts. You see, to make the Word of God the final authority means you choose the Word over everything else. You choose to align yourself with the Word of God in spite of everything you see or feel.

When I was just shy of 20 years old, before I was in full-time ministry, I worked as an assistant golf professional at a golf course for about six years. On November 7, 2003, when I was 21 years old, I heard the Lord call me into ministry. During this time, I was learning a lot about the Word of God and learning a lot about living by faith. The golf course opened up very early in the morning, and I worked the counter. Often times, early in the morning, I had a lot of downtime, so I would take my Bible and study while I waited for people to start arriving at the golf course. One morning, I was working and feeling disappointed about something I had done the day before, an action that I knew did not please the Lord. I was disappointed in myself because I was struggling to obey the Lord in this certain area. It seemed like I kept making the same mistake over and over again. It seemed to me like I could not get free. Well, early that morning the Lord spoke to my heart and told me to turn to Romans 6:22. That verse says, "But now being made free from sin, and become servants to

God, you have your fruit unto holiness, and the end everlasting life." As I read that verse, the Lord said to me, "When is now?"

I said, "Well, now is now."

He said, "That's right, now is now, and I said in that verse now being made free from sin, and so you are free from sin right now. Now is not tomorrow, now is not when you quit missing it in this area, now is right now." Right then, I made the Word of God the final authority in my life and I elevated it about everything else.

I said, "Okay, the Word of God says I'm free from sin so I must be." Now, at that moment, if I were to ask my feelings if I was free, they would have said no, you are not free. If I would have asked my eyes if I was free, they would have said no, you are not free. If I were to ask the devil if I was free, he would have said no, you are not free. But I wasn't asking my feelings, I wasn't asking my eyes, and I certainly wasn't asking the devil if I was free. The Word of God said I was free, so I said I must be free. I could have said I wasn't free because I didn't look free or feel free, but that would have been elevating what I saw and felt above the Word. You see, I made the Word of God the final authority in my life. This is a vital component to experiencing victory in a troubled time.

GRASSHOPPERS, TALL WALLS & BIG GIANTS

In the book of Exodus, after the days of Joseph, God's people were slaves to the Egyptians for 400 years. God raised up Moses because God wanted to lead His people out of Egyptian bondage and into the Promised Land.

God had spoken to His people about the Promised Land and

had told them that they would go in and possess it. In Exodus 23:23, 28 and 30, God said to them,

Mine Angel shall go before thee and bring thee in unto the Amorites, the Hittites, the Perizzites, the Canaanites, the Hivites, and the Jebusites: and I will cut them off. I will send hornets before thee, which shall drive out the Hivite, the Canaanite, and the Hittite, from before thee. By little and little I will drive them out from before thee, until thou be increased and inherit the land.

That right there is God's Word on the matter of them possessing the land. They should have taken that Word and made it the final authority in their lives.

When God's people got on the outskirts of the Promised Land, Moses sent twelve spies into the land to spy it out and come back and give a report. In Numbers 13:25–33, it tells us what they said:

They returned from searching of the land after forty days. And they went and came to Moses, and to Aaron, and to all the congregation of the children of Israel, unto the wilderness of Paran, to Kadesh; and brought back word unto them, and unto all the congregation, and showed them the fruit of the land. **And they told him, and said,** "We came unto the land whither thou sentest us, and surely it floweth with milk and honey; and this is the fruit of it. Nevertheless the people be strong that dwell in the land, and the cities are walled, and very great: and moreover we saw the children of Anak there. The Amalekites dwell in the land of the south: and the Hittites, and the Jebusites, and the Amorites, dwell in the mountains: and the Canaanites dwell by the sea, and by the coast of the Jordan." **And Caleb stilled the people before Moses,**

and said, "Let us go up at once, and possess it; for we are well able to overcome it." **But the men that went up with him said,** "We be not able to go up against the people; for they are stronger than we." **And they brought up an evil report of the land which they had searched unto the children of Israel, saying,** "The land, through which we have gone to search it, is a land that eateth up the inhabitants thereof; and all the people that we saw in it are men of a great stature. And there we saw the giants, the sons of Anak, which come of the giants: and we were in our own sight as grasshoppers, and so we were in their sight."

In this account, you have two groups of people. One group had made the Word of God final authority in their lives and one had not. The ten spies said they could not go in because they saw giants in the land, because they saw tall walls fortifying the land, and because they felt like grasshoppers. They elevated what they saw and felt above the Word of God. God had already told them in Exodus 23 that He would cause them to possess the land. However, they chose to elevate what they saw, how they felt and their own understanding above what God had said to them. God's Word was not their final authority. They didn't align themselves with the Word of God. They had elevated other things over the Word of God.

Joshua and Caleb, on the other hand, made God's Word the final authority in their lives. They saw the same giants, they saw the same walls, and were most likely having some of the same feelings that the others were having, but they chose to elevate what God said over everything else. They chose to make God's Word final authority in their lives. Even though they saw big giants and tall walls, they said, "Let us go up at once and possess it for we are well able to overcome it." They aligned themselves with the Word of God in spite of what they saw and felt. They eventually went in and possessed the Promised Land, and it was because they made God's Word the final authority in their lives. The others died in the wilderness. They missed God's good plan for their lives because they would not make His Word the final authority in their lives. If we want to enjoy God's good plan for our lives, we must make His Word our final authority.

They were staring trouble in the face. There were walls and giants standing between them and what God promised them. The reason they overcame and enjoyed victory was because they made God's Word the final authority in their lives.

You might be in a similar situation today to that of Joshua and Caleb. You may be staring trouble in the face. You may be under great attack in your body. You may be experiencing strong symptoms of anxiety and depression. You may be staring financial doom in the face. There may be all kinds of things standing between you and what God has promised you. If you will find out what God has to say in His Word about your situation and make it the final authority in your life, you can enjoy a great victory just like Joshua and Caleb did!

THANK YOU GENE HACKMAN

The following is a lesson I learned early on in my life from watching the movie, Hoosiers. Hoosiers is a movie about a small-town high school basketball team in Indiana with a new coach, played by Gene Hackman. It was one of my favorite movies growing up. In the movie, Gene Hackman plays a no-nonsense authoritative coach. One of the rules he put in place was that they needed to pass the ball four times on offense before they took a shot. Well, as you might imagine, one player on the team did not follow that rule. After the game, Gene Hackman said to the group, "What I say when it comes to this basketball team is the law, absolutely and without discussion."

When it comes to our lives and the situations we are facing, what God says is the law, absolutely and without discussion. If He said the land is yours and that you are to go in and possess it, then that is the law. It doesn't matter if there are walls surrounding that land and giants inhabiting that land. You are well able to possess that land and overcome the giants because what God says is the law, absolutely and without discussion.

God's Word has the final say in our lives. We don't ask our feelings if the Word of God is true. We don't ask our eyes if the Word of God is true. We don't ask our heads if the Word of God is true. If God says it, that settles it. His Word is the final authority in our lives and it is without dispute. If He says I have His joy, then His joy I have, whether I feel like I do or not. If He says I have His peace, then His peace I have, whether I feel like I do or not. If He says He will never leave me nor forsake me, then that is true even if it feels like God is a million miles away. This principle of making His Word final authority in your life is the launching pad from which you can launch your faith in Him and experience victory in troubled times.

GOD'S WORD IS RIGHT, GOD'S WORD IS TRUTH

There are two realities you must come to before you make God's Word the final authority in your life. You must come to the reality that God's Word is right and that God's Word is truth. Psalm 33:4 says, "For the Word of the Lord is right." Psalm 119:160 says, "Thy word is true from the beginning." God's Word is right. God's Word is true. Say that out loud. "God's Word is right. God's Word is true." If His Word is right, then anything that contradicts His Word is wrong. If His Word is true, then anything that contradicts His Word is false. Once you acknowledge those realities, then you are in position to make His Word the final authority in your life. Everyone wants to govern their life by what is right and what is true. Once we acknowledge that God's Word is the standard of right and truth, it will inspire us to then make it our final authority, and in turn, govern our lives according to it.

You see, that morning at the golf course, it was neither right nor true that I was bound by sin and could not get free. That was what the enemy was trying to tell me, and that was wrong and that was a lie because it contradicted the Word of God. I had already come to the reality that the Word of God was right and true, so it was very easy for me to make God's Word the final authority in my life regarding that situation. Until you acknowledge that God's Word is right and God's Word is truth, you will never make His Word the final authority in your life.

CHOOSE HIS WORD OVER EVERYTHING ELSE

Matthew 14 records the account of Peter walking on the water to go to Jesus. Verses 28–31 say,

And Peter answered him and said, "Lord, if it be thou, bid me come unto thee on the water." And he said, "Come." And when Peter was come down out of the ship, he walked on the water, to go to Jesus. But when he saw the wind boisterous, he was afraid; and beginning to sink, he cried, saying, "Lord, save me." And immediately Jesus stretched forth his hand, and caught him, and said unto him, "O thou of little faith, wherefore didst thou doubt?"

In this account, God's Word in regards to Peter walking on the water was "come." In that one word, God gave Peter the authority and ability to walk on that water no matter what came against him and tried to stop him. That word come should have been the final authority in Peter's life in regards to walking on that water. However, Peter saw the wind, and he chose to elevate the wind over God's Word. The enemy, through the wind, was telling Peter you are going to fall and you are going to drown, and Peter chose to elevate that over the Word. Peter could have spoken back to the wind and said, "I don't care how loud you are or how strong you blow, I have God's Word on it that I can walk on this water, so I elevate God's Word over the wind, over what I see and over how I feel." That would have been making God's Word final authority in that situation. However, as you know, Peter did not do that.

When Jesus saved Peter from drowning, He asked him a question. He said, "O thou of little faith, wherefore didst thou

47

doubt?" From a natural perspective, Peter had some pretty sound reasons to doubt. He could have said to Jesus, "Well, I doubted because I have never walked on the water, and before tonight, I had never seen anybody walk on water. Not only is it the middle of the night, but the wind was blowing hard. The waves were picking up. I can't swim, and there's no telling what kind of sea creatures are in this water." Jesus was so matter of fact in his question, "Why did you doubt?" that it leaves us with the idea that from Jesus' perspective, Peter had no reason to doubt. You see, God expects us to choose His Word over everything else. He expects us to elevate His Word over what we see, what we feel and over our natural understanding. In Jesus' eyes, Peter had no business choosing to elevate what the wind was saying over that one word from God, "come."

No matter what you are facing today, God expects you to make His Word the final authority and elevate His Word over everything else. If you are facing financial struggles today, God expects you to elevate His Word over everything else. Philippians 4:19 says, "My God shall supply all your need according to His riches in glory by Christ Jesus." God expects you to elevate that Word over what you see, over how you feel and over what your circumstances are saying. In the face of bills piling up, being laid off and not having enough money to keep your lights on, God expects you to align yourself with His Word and say, "My God will meet all my needs. He is my provider and I will not lack in my life. I will have more than enough money to do everything I need to do, and I will have a bunch left over to be a blessing to other people." When you do that, you are choosing His Word over everything else. You are making His Word your final authority.

If you are battling sickness and disease today, God expects you to make His Word final authority and elevate it above everything else. Matthew 8:17 says, "He Himself took our infirmities, and bare our sicknesses." Galatians 3:13 says, "Christ has redeemed us from the curse of the law being made a curse for us." Deuteronomy 28 reveals to us that sickness and disease is included in the curse that we are redeemed from. God expects you to align yourself with His Word. With symptoms of sickness and disease all over your body, He expects you to declare, "Jesus took my infirmities and bore my sicknesses. Therefore, I refuse to be sick. I refuse to bow my knee to sickness and disease. I call my body healed right now in Jesus name! Jesus has redeemed me from the curse of sickness and disease. Therefore, I say I am redeemed from sickness and disease." When you do that, you are elevating His Word over what you see and how you feel. You are making His Word the final authority in your life. You are believing His Word, decreeing His Word and acting like His Word is true in spite of what you see or how you feel. This is how you win!

You may be dealing with symptoms of anxiety and depression today. God expects you to find out what He has to say about anxiety and depression in His Word and then make it the final authority in your life. In regards to anxiety, in John 14:27, Jesus said, "Peace I leave with you, my peace I give unto you: not as the world giveth, give I unto you. Let not your heart be troubled, neither let it be afraid." Philippians 4:6 says, "Be anxious for nothing." In regards to sorrow and depression, in John 15:11, Jesus said, "These things have I spoken unto you, that my joy might remain in you, and that your joy might be full." Philippians 4:4 says, "Rejoice in the Lord always: and again, I say rejoice." You may have symptoms of anxiety all over you, but if you want to walk in victory, you have to elevate the Word of God over what you see and feel. You have to believe and decree, "Jesus has given me His peace, therefore I have it. I may not see His peace or feel His peace right now, but I have His peace. His peace is working in me right now. His peace passes all understanding, and therefore, I refuse to bow my knee to anxiety. I refuse to let my heart be troubled. I refuse to let my heart be afraid. I choose to be anxious for nothing!" You may have all the symptoms of depression in your life, but if you want to get free from it, you have to make God's Word the final authority in your life. You have to believe and decree, "I have Jesus' joy living in me right now, and therefore, my joy is full. I am full of the joy of the Lord. I am anointed with the oil of joy and gladness. Therefore, according to the Word, I make the choice to rejoice. I will rejoice and I will be glad!"

What I am describing to you in these examples is what it looks like to make God's Word the final authority in your life. All of us will experience challenges in our lives. All of us will deal with symptoms of some kind. All of us will face negative circumstances. When we do, if we want to experience victory, we have to choose to make God's Word the final authority in our lives. Your victory in troubled times starts right here with making God's Word final authority in your life. This is how you win! This is how you overcome!

A KEY TO VICTORY

When you make God's Word final authority in your life, it will lead to your victory. One big mistake many people make is that while they know what the Word says, they fail to govern their lives by what the Word says. They do not make the Word of God the final authority in their lives.

God's Word is alive and full of power. Hebrews 4:12, in The Amplified Bible, says, "For the Word that God speaks is alive and full of power." However, until you make God's Word the final authority in your life and govern your life by the Word, you will not see the power of God's Word working in your life.

The power of God's Word only works in the lives of people who govern their lives by it. You have to believe the Word, act on the Word and align yourself with the Word if you want to see the Word work in your life.

Over the years I've heard people quote John 8:32 and say, "The truth will make you free." That is a partial quote of something Jesus said, but not the whole quote. In John 8:31, Jesus said, "If you continue in my Word, then are you my disciples indeed; And you shall know the truth, and the truth shall make you free." The truth of God's Word is not making everybody free. The truth of God's Word is not even making all believers free. The truth of God's Word will only make those free who continue in the Word, those who govern their lives by the Word. When you make the Word the final authority in your life, you position yourself to see the power of that Word work and produce victory right in the middle of troubled times!

CHAPTER 3

GET YOUR MOUTH IN GEAR

When it comes to experiencing victory in troubled times, the words you choose to speak are absolutely critical. In fact, I would go so far as to say that if you do not get it right where your words are concerned, victory in troubled times is an impossibility. You will see, throughout this chapter, a number of people in the Bible in high-pressure situations use their words and experience victory. If you want to experience victory in troubled times, you must get your mouth in gear!

LIFE & DEATH IS IN THE POWER OF THE TONGUE

God has made it very clear to us in His Word that our words are significant and powerful. Proverbs 18:21 says, "Death and life are in the power of the tongue." Often, when we think of death and life, we think only about living physically or dying physically. When we hear life, the tendency is to think of someone being alive.

When we hear death, the tendency is to think of someone being dead. Certainly, it is correct to use life and death in those terms. However, the reality is that both life and death are working forces that produce certain things. Life is a force that causes things to be strong, to thrive and to flourish. Death is a force that works to weaken, decay and destroy. When you see someone alive, strong and active in this life, the force of life is producing that. When you see a person's body lying in the casket, the force of death produced that. Death was at work in their body, causing it to weaken, decay and then eventually be destroyed.

Working at a golf course for a half-dozen years, I developed a fondness for green grass and well-manicured landscaping. In the middle of spring, the grass is bright green, the trees are bright green and generally most of the flowers and plants at that time are in full bloom. Life is the force that produces all of that, and it is absolutely beautiful. However, by the time late fall comes around, the grass begins to turn brown, the leaves fall off of the trees and the springtime plants die. That is the force of death at work.

Life and death are spiritual forces that will work in any area of your life. The force of life can work in any area of your life and cause that area to be strong, to thrive and to flourish. On the other end, the force of death can work in any area of your life and cause that area to weaken, decay and be destroyed. For instance, the force of life can work in your marriage and cause your marriage to be strong, to thrive and to flourish — a place where you and your spouse have a great relationship, you love each other and enjoy each other to the utmost. The opposite is true as well. The force of death can work in your marriage causing your marriage to weaken, to decay and to be destroyed. That force of death can work and produce strife and bitterness in your marriage to the point of divorce. The force of life can work in your finances causing you to be strong financially. It can work so powerfully in your finances that it causes you to have more than enough to fulfill all your financial responsibilities, enjoy nice amenities in your life and be a tremendous blessing to other people. Again, on the other end, the force of death can work in your finances. That force of death can cause you to be weak and struggle financially to the place where you don't have enough provision to even take care of your own financial responsibilities. We need to renew our minds to the reality that both life and death are working forces that produce.

The scripture in Proverbs 18:21 says, "Death and life are in the power of the tongue." Therefore, the working of these forces in your life is in the control of the tongue. You can choose to speak words that will put the force of life to work in your life, or you can choose to speak words that will put the force of death to work in your life. The words you choose to speak determine which of these forces are at work in your situation and in your life. If you speak God's Words in the midst of a troubled time, that will put the force of life to work. That force of life will work to bring you out of that low place, out of that troubled time, and produce victory in your life. If you speak words that contradict God's Words in the midst of a pressured situation, then you put the force of death to work. That force of death will work to keep you low, keep you down and produce defeat in your life.

If you are in the midst of a trying time, if you are in a low place, if you are facing a seemingly impossible situation, you need the force of life working in your situation. You need that force of life working to bring you out of that low place and into a place of prosperity and victory. If you have the force of death at work in your situation, you don't stand a chance and victory is an impossibility. If you choose to speak words that are in opposition to God's words, that puts the force of death to work in your life and you will not experience victory. However, if you will choose to speak words that put the force of life to work, you can experience victory in a troubled time!

I WILL NOT FEAR

In 2011, the enemy was attacking me in a lot of different areas. One thing I began to experience were some very real symptoms of anxiety and depression. I'm not going to go into great detail about those symptoms because I don't feel the need, on this occasion, to shine light on the devil's work. However, I will tell you that what I was experiencing, I had never experienced before. Just as a point of note, a few years after these attacks, the Lord showed me that I had gotten into that situation because there were some things He had shown me to do (and not to do) that I got sloppy with and let slip. All that being said, back in 2011 I was experiencing these symptoms and they were very, very real.

At that time, I had been in ministry for close to eight years and had been walking very closely with the Lord for those eight years. Throughout that time, God had taught me a lot about living by faith and experiencing victory in my life. The things He taught me I had put into practice and seen them work in my own life. As a result, I was enjoying victory over the enemy. However, I had let some of those principles slip. I had gotten sloppy and wasn't doing the things I knew to do. The things I had seen work for me, I let them slip. One day, in a time of prayer, the Lord told me, "Dance with the one who brung you." I knew in my heart that He was telling me to go back to the things that had gotten me this far. Go back to the principles of faith that you have learned and seen work in your life. I did just that. I got back on the Word of God, back on the principles of faith, and enjoyed a great victory, very quickly, over those symptoms I was experiencing. I'm thrilled to announce to you that I haven't had a problem with those things since.

One day, in the middle of all those symptoms, I had a breakthrough moment spiritually. I did not realize how important it was until years later. I was experiencing some very strong symptoms of fear and anxiety, so I went outside to pray. We live on a hill in the country that is covered with beautiful foliage. A creek runs behind our house. It is a wonderful setting to go outside and pray. Well, I did that. I had symptoms of fear all over me. It was fear so real that I could feel it all over my spirit, soul and body. It was the kind of fear that tries to grip you and paralyze you on the inside. It was the kind of fear that makes you nauseous inside. It was the tormenting spirit of fear and it was not from God! Outside of our house, on the side closest to the woods, with those symptoms crawling all over me, I shouted as loud as I possibly could and with all the strength I had, "I will not fear!" I chose to say that because I knew God told me in His Word to fear not. I knew God told me in John 14 to not let my heart be afraid. I knew God told me in His Word that He had not given me the spirit of fear. By the grace of God and with the help of the Holy Spirit, I refused to bow my knee to fear, and instead chose to say about me what God said about me. I got my mouth in gear!

After experiencing those symptoms for months, I enjoyed a very quick victory over those things, and it was directly connected to the words I chose to speak. When I spoke those words, I put the force of life to work in my spirit and in my mind. Through that force, God completely delivered me from fear, anxiety and depression. It was the force of life that caused me to be strong, to thrive and to flourish in my spirit and mind. That force was put to work by the words I chose to speak. When I spoke those words, God brought about a great victory in my life.

A DECLARATION IN DISTRESS

Psalm 23 is a very familiar psalm to many people. It says,

The Lord is my shepherd; I shall not want. 2 He maketh me to lie down in green pastures: he leadeth me beside the still waters. 3 He restoreth my soul: he leadeth me in the paths of righteousness for his name's sake. 4 Yea, though I walk through the valley of the shadow of death, I will fear no evil: for thou art with me; thy rod and thy staff they comfort me. 5 Thou preparest a table before me in the presence of mine enemies: thou anointest my head with oil; my cup runneth over. 6 Surely goodness and mercy shall follow me all the days of my life: and I will dwell in the house of the Lord forever.

David wrote this psalm in a time of great distress. In fact, he wrote this psalm in the valley of the shadow of death. Verse 4 says,

"Yea, though I walk through the valley of the shadow of death…"
This psalm was penned when David was in a low place, a dark place,
a troubled time. In a Hebrew commentary entitled, "Tehillim," I
found this commentary note about Psalm 23. It says,

David composed this famed psalm during one of the most
dangerous and discouraging times in his life. He was a forlorn
fugitive, fleeing from King Saul and his army. In desperation, David
hid himself in a barren, desolate forest called Hareth, named so
because it was parched and dry like baked earthenware.

To really appreciate this psalm, it is imperative that you gain
concept of the place from which David wrote it. David was right
in the middle of a very high-pressure situation when he wrote this
psalm.

The other thing we need to lay hold of in talking about Psalm
23 is that it is a declaration of faith. The psalm is a statement of
faith. David is in a barren and desolate place. There is no food to
eat. There is no water to drink. There are no restaurants, hotels or
grocery stores around the corner. He is staring death in the face, and
he looks right back on death and makes this awesome declaration of
faith. In the middle of a troubled time, he used his words!

This psalm is a declaration in distress. David was not just
writing something, he was saying something. In this troubled time,
in this pressure situation, David got his mouth in gear and made a
declaration of faith based on his covenant with God. When all he
could see with his eyes was scarcity and lack, he said, "The Lord is
my shepherd I will not lack." When there wasn't a green pasture in
sight, he said, "God makes me to lie down in green pastures." When

there was no fresh drinking water to be found anywhere, he said, "God leads me beside still waters." When he had every reason to be tired and weary in his soul, he said, "The Lord restores my soul." When he didn't know where to go or what to do, he said, "God leads me on paths of righteousness for his name's sake." When fear was all around him and trying to come all over him, he said, "Yea, though I walk through the valley of the shadow of death, I will fear no evil." When defeat seemed to be inevitable, he said, "My God will prepare a table before me in the presence of my enemies." When abundance was as far away as the moon, he said, "My cup runs over." When the goodness of God and the mercy of God were unseen by the natural eye, he said, "Surely your goodness and mercy will follow me all the days of my life." David was not saying what he saw. David was not saying what he felt. To do that, he would have had to speak in opposition to the covenant God made with him. David made a declaration of faith in distress. In his darkest hour, his faith in God shined the brightest, and you can see his faith in what he said.

When we stay in faith and align our words with God's Words, it positions us to see God move on our behalf. You see, God works in our lives through our faith. It started in salvation. Ephesians 2:8 says, "For by grace you are saved through faith." God saved us by His wonderful grace, but He did it through our faith. God cannot save a person by His grace if they will not believe. Without a person's faith, God has no access into their lives to do what He wants to do.

In Matthew 13, Jesus went to his hometown to teach, preach and heal. In verse 58 it says, "He did not many mighty works there because of their unbelief." Mark 6:5 says, "He could there do no mighty work." The reason was because without faith, God has no access to move in our lives by His wonderful grace.

David staying in faith and making this declaration of faith in this troubled time positioned him to see God do great and mighty things in his life. Now, the "Tehillim" commentary goes on to say,

God did not forsake David. He soaked this dry forest with moisture, which had the flavor of the World to Come, making even the grass and the leaves of the forest succulent and edible. This showed David that God supports and nourishes at all times even when the chances of survival seem to be non-existent.

It is their belief that God moved on David's behalf in such a way that He turned that barren, desolate forest into a thriving, green and succulent forest with vegetation and water. That should be no shock to us because in Isaiah 43:19, God said, "Behold, I will do a new thing; not it shall spring forth; shall you not know it? I will even make a way in the wilderness and rivers in the desert." Whatever you believe God did for David in Psalm 23, you have to acknowledge that David did not die in the valley of the shadow of death. Instead, God made a way for him and gave him a great victory in his life. I personally believe the "Tehillim" commentary. I believe that God moved on David's behalf in a mighty way, in complete accordance with what David declared in Psalm 23. The big thing we need to lay hold of is that in this pressure place, David used his words and got his mouth in gear!

How about you? How about me? When we are in a pressure place, does what we say have anything to do with whether or not we are victorious? The answer, a thousand times over, is yes! It does matter what we say if we desire to experience victory in troubled times. If we are facing a troubled time, and talk our feelings, talk the problem and talk what we see, we will not enjoy victory. We will not overcome. We have to do exactly what David did. We have to speak words of faith when we can't see a way out. We have to speak words of faith when we don't feel like anything good is ever going to come out of this situation. We have to speak words of faith when we don't understand. We have to speak words of faith in the low spot, in the dark place, in the midst of the trying time. If we will, God can move on our behalf!

YOUR LIFE & YOUR MOUTH

There is a direct connection between what you believe and what you say and what you experience in your life. This is a connection that many people never make. In Mark 11:23, Jesus said, "For verily I say unto you, That whosoever shall say unto this mountain, Be thou removed, and be thou cast into the sea; and shalt not doubt in his heart, but shall believe that those things which he says shall come to pass; he shall have whatsoever he says." According to the Master, if you say something and believe that what you say will come to pass, you will have what you say. This works on both the positive and the negative side. You can say something negative and have what you say. You can say something positive and have what you say.

In regards to the first generation of the Children of Israel, who were delivered from Egyptian bondage, you had two groups of people saying two different things about going in and possessing the Promised Land. One group of people believed and said, "We cannot possess the land." Joshua and Caleb believed and said, "We are well able to overcome it." The simple reality is that both groups of people experienced in life exactly what they believed and what they said. Joshua and Caleb eventually went in and possessed the land. The other group of people never possessed the land and died in the wilderness. You can see clearly from these verses that there is a direct connection between what you say and what you experience in your life.

Psalm 34:12-13 says, "What man is he that desires life and loves many days, that he may see good? Keep your tongue from evil." The Lord is asking us a question in this verse. The Living Bible, in verse 34 says, "Do you want a long good life?" I believe most everybody would emphatically answer yes to that question. God then tells us that if we want a long good life, we must keep our mouths from speaking bad things. Well, what does your mouth have to do with the kind of life you enjoy? Everything! Proverbs 13:3 says, "He that keeps his mouth keeps his life: but he that opens wide his lips shall have destruction." Here is yet another verse revealing to us that what we experience in our lives is directly connected to what we say. Your life and your lips are connected. Proverbs 18:21 in The Century English Version says, "You will eat everything you say." The International Children's Bible says, "What You say affects how you live." James 3:6 says, "[The tongue] starts a fire that influences all of life." Words have a far-reaching effect. They can and will affect every area of your life. Good words will have a good effect. Bad words will have a bad effect. If you believe the Bible, then you believe your words affect your life.

AN OPEN-NOTE QUIZ & A BAD CONFESSION

I learned this lesson early on in my walk with the Lord. Back in the early 2000s, right after I knew the Lord was calling me into ministry, one of the first things He taught me was about the power of my words. In fact, He began to lead me to the same scriptures I have been sharing with you in this chapter. After the Lord showed me these things, I endeavored to put them into practice the best I knew how.

I was going to Southern Illinois University at Edwardsville back then and studying to get my teaching degree in kinesiology. Do not be too impressed with that word kinesiology. It is just a fancy way of saying I was studying to be a physical education teacher.

One day, me and around half a dozen of my classmates were sitting together around a table in the commons area before class. Earlier that week, our teacher had given us an assignment. He had told us to answer 25 questions that were in the textbook and write the answers down in our notebook and bring it the following day to class. He told us that we were going to have an open-note quiz with only two questions that he would randomly select from the 25 questions he gave us as a homework assignment. He encouraged us that if we did the homework and answered all 25 questions, this quiz would be as simple as copying the two answers from our notes. Well, guess who didn't do their homework and answer all 25 questions? That's correct, yours truly. There were two questions, for whatever reason, that I did not take the time to answer. As I was sitting out there in the commons area with my classmates, I said, "You watch, one of the questions I didn't answer will be on the quiz." I almost cringe right now as I recall this story, to think I said something so foolish. There was about a one-in-twelve chance that one of those questions was on the test. Those were pretty slim odds. I should have been safe, but the power of my words was working against me.

We all headed upstairs to our classroom. All the wise students who answered all the questions were feeling confident and comfortable. To them, this was going to be the easiest quiz they had ever taken. I was neither confident nor comfortable. Not only that, my words were working against me and I didn't know it! The whole time walking up the stairs, I was hoping that the questions that I failed to answer would not be on the quiz. The problem was, I had already believed and spoke. What I wanted to happen did not match what I said. We walked into the classroom and we all sat down. The teacher greeted us and chatted with us for a few minutes. Then he randomly selected two questions that would be on the quiz. I believe he might even have drawn the numbers out of a hat. One of the questions that I didn't answer was one of the questions he "randomly" selected. The Lord spoke to my heart and reminded me what I said to my classmates before class. He told me, "Son, there is power in your words." There was a direct connection between what I believed and said, and what I experienced in my life.

A THOUSAND DOLLAR CHECK

That was a story about the negative effect of my words, so let me share with you a story when my words worked for my good. I heard the call of God to go into ministry on November 7th, 2003.

I immediately enrolled in Bible school, and God opened up a door for me to be an associate pastor at a small church in a town about ten minutes from where I lived. From 2003 to early 2007, I was in ministry part time. I was finishing up college. I was a substitute teacher in the winter, and I worked at a golf course through the spring, summer and fall.

In March of 2007, I was at Kenneth Copeland's Victory Campaign in Branson, Missouri, at Keith Moore's church. On March 8, 2007, at the end of the Thursday night service, Brother Copeland had us all stand up, and when I stood up, the Lord spoke to me and said, "I'm calling you into full-time ministry. You say, 'What about money?' I say, the Blessing. You say, 'What about opportunities to preach?' I say, the Blessing. You say, 'What about finances?' I say, the Blessing. The Year of the open door. You have to walk through the door. I will not push you through. As you walk through the door, the Blessing will work to produce the opportunities for you. The Blessing is in the way, and if you don't get in the way, the Blessing can't produce for you. You've said, 'I know where God's calling me, but I don't know how to get there.' Your answer is the Blessing. The Blessing will make a way where it looks like there is no way. The Blessing is how you make that dream in your heart become a reality in your life. You go and take that dream that I've placed in your heart, and it will manifest everywhere you go because of the Blessing. Don't wait another second. Go now. Don't wait another second. Go now."

After hearing from the Lord like that, I quickly made the decision that I was going into ministry full time just as soon as I got back home. When I got back home, I met with my boss at the golf course, put in my two weeks notice and that was that. I was going into full-time ministry.

Now, at that time, I was having services on Sunday mornings with a small group of people. In January, February and March, Matthew Allaria Ministries had around $1,000 a month come in. As you might guess, that is not enough to cover all of your expenses and pay a full-time employee. However, I stepped out in faith, and in April, May and June, the income tripled. However, in July, things started to get a little tight, and we were in need of income.

One day, I was in the car praying, fellowshipping with the Lord and speaking God's Word over the finances of the ministry. As I did, I heard this come out of my mouth, "Someone is going to give a thousand-dollar check into this ministry." When I said it, I knew it was from the Lord, so I said it again. "Someone is going to give a thousand-dollar check into this ministry." What was I doing? I was saying what God said to me and using my words in a high-pressure situation.

A few weeks later, after I had finished with one of our Sunday morning services, I went behind the curtain and found a card, with my name on it, laying on my briefcase. I opened up the card; it was from a couple whose son was really being ministered to through the ministry. Well, inside the card there was a thousand-dollar check written to MAM! I was exceedingly thankful to the Lord and beyond excited! In that instance, I saw my words work for my good!

GET THE WORDS OF VICTORY IN YOUR MOUTH

If you want to experience victory in troubled times, the words you choose to speak are absolutely vital. If what you experience in life is directly connected to your words and you want to experience victory in troubled times, then you need to get victory words in your mouth.

Jesus taught us that we would have what we believed and what we said. Well, you cannot have victory if you speak defeat. You cannot have healing if you talk sickness. You cannot have peace and joy if you talk anxiety and depression. You have to get God's Word in your mouth. You have to get the words of victory in your mouth. I would echo what God said to us in Psalm 34:12. Do you want to experience victory in troubled times? Do you want to overcome that obstacle? Do you want to triumph in a time of pressure? Then get the words of victory in your mouth!

Anybody can talk about how hard it is or how bad they feel, but champions of faith will talk the Word when the pressure is the greatest. Champions of faith will speak words of faith in the midst of darkness and despair. It is easy to talk the problem and talk what you see and talk how you feel. However, it takes some spiritual gumption and fortitude to speak words of faith when defeat seems inevitable. Only the ones who do this will experience victory in troubled times.

USING YOUR WORDS

In a troubled time, in a time when we are under attack, we can use our words like a weapon to accomplish things. Let's look at some verses in the eleventh chapter of the book of Mark. Mark 11:12–23 says,

When they were come from Bethany, he was hungry: 13 And seeing a fig tree afar off having leaves, he came, if haply he might find anything thereon: and when he came to it, he found nothing but leaves; for the time of figs was not yet. 14 And Jesus answered and said unto it, "No man eat fruit of thee hereafter forever." And his disciples heard it. 15 And they come to Jerusalem 19 And when evening was come, he went out of the city. 20 And in the morning, as they passed by, they saw the fig tree dried up from the roots. 21 And Peter calling to remembrance saith unto him, "Master, behold, the fig tree which thou cursed is withered away." 22 Jesus answering saith unto them, "Have faith in God. 23 For verily I say unto you, that whosoever shall say unto this mountain, Be thou removed, and be thou cast into the sea; and shall not doubt in his heart, but shall believe that those things which he saith shall come to pass; he shall have whatsoever he saith."

Jesus and his disciples were walking from Bethany to the temple and Jesus was hungry. He saw a fig tree and was going to get some figs to eat, but he did not find any on the tree. Jesus spoke to the tree and said, "No man eat fruit of you hereafter forever." Afterwards, they continued on to the temple. This just so happened to be the day when Jesus overturned the tables of the money changers in the temple. That night, they headed back to Bethany to sleep. The next morning, they were headed back to the temple, and Peter noticed that the tree Jesus had spoken to was withered away. When Peter mentioned it to Jesus, Jesus responded by telling them they could use their words and their faith and move mountains (verses 22-23).

The context of these verses is that Jesus is teaching them (and us) to use their words and their faith to accomplish things. Most people, when they think about speaking, they don't think about using their words to accomplish something. Most think only about using their words to communicate their thoughts and feelings with other people. In the world, we are not taught to speak to things and use our words to accomplish things. In a lot of churches, believers are not taught to use their words to accomplish things. Yet, here in these verses, we have the Master teaching us that we can use our words and our faith and see things change in our lives. We can use our words and our faith to overcome challenges. We can use our words and our faith to see victory in troubled times.

Joshua used his words to accomplish things. Joshua 10:12–13 says,

Then spoke Joshua to the Lord in the day when the Lord delivered up the Amorites before the children of Israel, and he said in the sight of Israel, "Sun, stand thou still upon Gibeon; and thou, Moon, in the valley of Ajalon" And the sun stood still, and the moon stayed, until the people had avenged themselves.

Joshua used his words and his faith to accomplish something. He spoke to something physical and saw it respond to his words. Well, if Joshua can use his words and faith and see things change, then why not you? Why not me?

When the disciples asked Jesus about the fig tree, He did not say, "Do not even think about trying this. Only I can use my words and faith and see things change." He said, "Whosoever shall say unto this mountain." Whosoever includes you! Whosoever includes me! The disciples were amazed by what Jesus did to the fig tree, and

Jesus told them, you can do this. You can use your words and faith and see things change in your life. In fact, in Luke 17:6, Jesus said to his disciples, "If you had faith as a grain of mustard seed, you might say unto this sycamine tree, Be though plucked up by the root and be thou planted in the sea; and it should obey you." Jesus is telling them, you can do what I did. You can use your words and your faith and see things change just like Jesus did.

ACT LIKE GOD

God used His Words to accomplish things. We see this in the very beginning of the book of Genesis when God used His Words to create the world and everything in it. Hebrews 11:3 says, "The worlds were framed by the Word of God." God used His Words to create and accomplish. In Isaiah 55:11, God said, "So shall my word be that goes forth out of my mouth: it shall not return unto me void, but it shall accomplish which I please." God did not just speak to communicate, He spoke to accomplish things. God spoke to affect and for effect. In Psalm 107:20 it says, "God sent His Word and healed them and delivered them from their destructions." Here again, we see God using His Words to accomplish something. When He wanted to heal and deliver His people, He used His Words to do it.

Jesus also used His words to accomplish things in His earthly life and ministry. That should be no surprise to us because in John 14:9, Jesus said, "He that has seen me has seen the Father." In John 5:19, Jesus said, "Verily, verily, I say unto you, The son can do nothing of himself, what he sees the Father do: for what things

71

soever he does, these the Son does likewise." Jesus is telling us that He only does what He sees the Father do. The reason Jesus used His words to accomplish things is because that is what He saw the Father do. Colossians 1:15, in The Amplified Bible says, "Now He is the exact likeness of the unseen God [the visible representation of the invisible]." In His earthly life, Jesus was the visible representation of the invisible God. Therefore, all throughout His ministry, we see the Master using His words to accomplish things. In the fourth chapter of the book of Mark, He and his disciples were in a boat and a great storm came. Mark 4:39 says, "He rebuked the wind, and said unto the sea, peace be still." Jesus used His words to accomplish something. In the fourth chapter of Luke, Peter's mother-in-law had a great fever. In verse 39 it says, "And he [Jesus] stood over her and rebuked the fever; and it left her." Jesus spoke to a fever. He used His words to accomplish something. In the eighth chapter of the book of Matthew, a leper came to Jesus and wanted to be healed. Verse 3 says, "Jesus put forth his hand, and touched him saying, I will; be thou clean. And immediately the leprosy was cleansed." Again, Jesus used His words to accomplish something. In Matthew 4, when Satan came and tempted Jesus three times, Jesus used His words to resist the devil and experience victory over him. Three times, Jesus opened His mouth and spoke the Word of God. He used His words to accomplish things. He used His words for effect. He used His words to affect.

Many will hear things like that and say, "Yeah, that was God using His Words and I am not God." Others will say, "Yeah, that was Jesus using His words and I am not Jesus." Well, we know that you are not God and we know you are not Jesus. However, we also know that the Bible tells us that we are to be imitators of God. Ephesians 5:1, in The Passion Translation, says, "Be imitators of God in everything you do." In The Century English Version it says, "Do as God does." We are supposed to imitate God. If He uses His Words to accomplish things, then we are supposed to put His Words in our mouths and use our words to accomplish things. 1 John 2:6 says, "He that says he abides in him [Jesus] ought himself also so to walk, even as he walked." The word walk in that verse means to conduct your life. If we are believers, then we should be endeavoring to conduct ourselves just as the Master conducted Himself; He used His Words to accomplish things. You too are supposed to use your words to accomplish things.

Not only do we see God using His Words to accomplish things and Jesus using His words to accomplish things, but we see "normal" people in the Bible using their words to accomplish things. We saw already how Joshua used his words to stop the sun and the moon. In Acts 3, Peter used his words to get the lame man at the gate healed. In Mark 5, the woman with the issue of blood used her words to receive her healing. She said, "If I may but touch his clothes, I shall be whole." David used his words in his fight against Goliath. It says in 1 Samuel 17:45–46,

Then said David to the Philistine, "Thou comes to me with a sword, and with a spear, and with a shield: but I come to thee in the name of the Lord of hosts, the God of the armies of Israel, whom thou hast defied. 46 This day will the Lord deliver you into my hand; and I will smite you, and take your head from you and

I will give the carcasses of the host of the Philistines this day unto the fowls of the air, and to the wild beasts of the earth."

In Daniel chapter 3, the three Hebrews were getting ready to be thrown into the fiery furnace because they would not bow down and worship Nebuchadnezzar's false god, and they used their words. They said in verse 17, "If it be so, our God whom we serve is able to deliver us from the burning fiery furnace, and he will deliver us out of your hand, O King." These people in scripture were using their words to accomplish things. If God used His Words to accomplish things, if Jesus used His words to accomplish things, and if people of faith in the Bible used their words to accomplish things, then you should use your words to accomplish things!

WORDS WORK

One big thing we must acknowledge about words is that they work. Words produce. Words accomplish. Every word you speak works to do something. Words that are spoken never do nothing. They always do something. That goes for every word you speak.

Proverbs 18:20 says, "A man's belly shall be satisfied with the fruit of his mouth and with the increase of his lips shall he be filled." The word fruit and the word increase both mean to produce. In fact, The New International Reader's Version says, "What their words produce can satisfy them." Words produce, words work and words accomplish.

In multiple scriptures, you see this phrase, "The fruit of the mouth." One place you find that is in Proverbs 13:2. What is the fruit of the mouth? Well, the fruit of the earth is what the earth produces. The fruit of the womb is what the womb produces. The fruit of a tree is what a tree produces. The fruit of the mouth is what the mouth produces. We need to renew our minds to the reality that every word we speak works. Every word we speak is doing something. The words that we speak do not do nothing. The words we speak work to produce things in our lives.

I have two beautiful daughters who love to play with the bubble machine at their grandma's house. When I grew up in the 80s there were no bubble machines. If you wanted a bubble, you had to blow a bubble through that little plastic tool they gave you with the bottle of bubbles. Anyone who has used one of those little tools knows that they produce the most pathetic little bubbles you have ever seen. Now, with that bubble machine, all you have to do is just flip the switch and that machine just starts blowing out bubbles. Our girls like to run and chase those bubbles. Those bubbles accomplish nothing. They just shoot out of that machine and float in the air for a little while and then they pop. That is how too many of us treat our words. Too often we act like our words do not matter, that our words do not have effect, but that's not true. Our words are not like those bubbles. Our words do not leave our mouths and just float in the air for a while and then pop, having no effect on anything in our lives. Our words have effect. Our words work. Every word we speak is working in our lives to help us or to hurt us.

One of the worst things you can do in a troubled time is to speak words that will hurt you and not help you. You are already under attack. You already have an adversary (the devil) who wants to steal, kill and destroy in your life. You already have the curse that is trying to work against you and destroy your life. You might even have people who are against you. You have enough things working against you. The last thing you need to do in a troubled time is to speak words that are working against you. It is vitally important in a pressure place, in a dark hour, in a low place, that we speak words that will help us and not hurt us. We need to speak words that push us towards victory and not towards defeat. We need to speak words that will give God access into our lives to do great and mighty things. We need to speak words that will shut the devil out of our lives. We need to speak words that will push us towards prosperity, deliverance and victory. We must refuse to speak words that will push us towards failure, bondage and defeat.

MY SWEET AMBER

Acknowledging the reality that our words produce should inspire us to purposefully use our words to accomplish things in our lives. If I believe that my words really do work, then I will speak words that work to produce good things in my life. If my words really do produce, then I am going to speak words that produce what I want in my life.

Shortly after I was called into ministry in 2003, I developed a strong desire to marry a godly woman. At that time in my life, it was one of my heart's greatest desires. I had learned about the power of my words, so I went to the Word of God and found out what God had to say about me having a godly wife. I then started speaking God's Word over my life, in regards to this situation. Here is a small portion of the declaration of faith I made about the woman I wanted to marry:

My wife comes from the Lord and because she comes from the Lord she is perfect for me and I for her (Prov. 19:14). I have a wife that is suitable, adapted, and complementary to me (Gen 2:18). I have a wife that is proper and fit for me (Gen 2:18). I have a wife that is able and qualified to be my wife (Gen 2:18). I have a wife that is wise, understanding, and prudent (Prov 19:14). I have a wife who acts intelligently and wisely (Prov 19:14). I have a virtuous wife – one who is strong in mind (Prov 31:10). I have a wife that I can safely trust in (Prov 31:11). I have a wife who will comfort and encourage me and do me good and not evil (Prov 31:12). I have a wife that will work willingly with her hands (Prov 31:13). I have a wife who is strong spiritually, mentally, and physically for her God-given task (Prov 31:17). I have a wife who is hungry for God's uncompromised Word and is constantly feeding on God's Word (Prov. 31:17). I have a wife who doesn't live in fear, but one who lives in the love of God (Prov. 37:21). I have a wife who carries herself with strength and dignity (Prov 31:25). I have a wife who is beautiful inside and out. I have a wife who I am attracted to physically as well as spiritually. I have a wife who is beautiful to my eye spiritually and physically (Prov 31:25). I have a wife who speaks wisdom in line with The Word of God and in line with the love of God (Prov 31:26). I have a wife who is strong in character (Prov 31:29). I have a wife that has placed God first in her life and is unwilling to compromise on His Word (Prov 31:30). My Father told me in His Word to not be unequally yoked together with unbelievers so I thank God that my wife is from God she is a believer and we are equally yoked together (2 Corinthians 6:14).

I have a wife who will submit herself to me and reverence me (Eph 5:22,33). I love my wife as Christ loved the church and gave himself for it (Eph 5:25).

When I made this declaration of faith, I was using my words to accomplish something. I was using my words for effect and to affect my life. I knew that words worked. I knew words produced. As a result, I spoke words that would produce what I wanted in my life. In giving me Amber, the Lord gave me a wife that was beyond anything that I could have ever asked for, hoped for, dreamed or imagined. Amber is everything that I declared about my wife and so much more than that. She is the Lord's greatest gift to me. I know the wife that I'm enjoying today is directly connected to the words that I spoke when I didn't have a wife.

THE ENEMY IS AFTER YOUR MOUTH

One thing you need to understand about your enemy is that he believes in the power of words. He believes in it so much that he is working night and day to get the wrong words in your mouth. Luke 11:53–54 says, "As he [Jesus] said these things unto them, the scribes and the Pharisees began to urge him vehemently, and to provoke him to speak of many things: Lying in wait for him and seeking to catch something out of his mouth that they might accuse him." Through these scribes and Pharisees, the enemy was prodding and poking Jesus, trying to get him to say the wrong thing. The enemy was trying to get Jesus to say something that was in opposition to the Word of God.

Satan is after your mouth because he knows apart from your words, he has no way into your life. In John 14:30, Jesus said, "The prince of this world cometh, and hath nothing in me." Jesus is revealing to us that the enemy had no way into his life. Satan had no point of entry, no access into Jesus' life. In Mark 4, Satan tried to kill Jesus with a hurricane and could not do it. In John 8, the enemy stirred up a crowd of angry people who wanted to stone Jesus, and when they tried, they were not successful. In Matthew 4, the enemy tempted Jesus to sin and was not successful. It is evident that Satan had no way into Jesus' life. One of the big reasons that was true is found in John 12:50. Jesus said, "Whatsoever I speak therefore, even as the Father said unto me, so I speak." Jesus only said what the Father told him to say. In his earthly life and ministry, no words ever came out of His mouth that contradicted God's Words. The enemy had no way into Jesus' life because he found no way into His mouth.

The enemy has to get his words into your mouth, elsewise he cannot operate in your life. He has to get you speaking words that are in opposition to God's Words. He has to get you talking your feelings, talking the problem and talking your circumstances. He has to get you speaking words of fear, doubt and unbelief. This is his only hope in your life, and as a result, he is desperate to get you to say the wrong things. He will bombard you with negative thoughts and feelings, endeavoring to get you to say the wrong thing so that he can have access into your life.

The cry of your heart must be that no matter how great the pressure is, no matter how trying your circumstances are, and no matter how hopeless your situation appears, you will not speak the utterances of your adversary. You will not speak words of doubt, fear and unbelief. You have to settle in your heart that you will only say what the Word of God says. You will say what God says and nothing else. You need to make this decision because the enemy is after your mouth.

GRANDPA WILL NEVER WALK AGAIN

I grew up in a rural area in Southern Illinois. I lived in the country the first 25 years of my life, and I am a country boy to this day. My grandparents lived just a couple miles from us on a farm. My grandpa had cattle, pigs, barns, tractors and some land that he farmed. Growing up as a young boy, I had a lot of fun at Grandma and Grandpa's house.

My grandpa was, and is to this day, what I would call a man's man. He was a working man. Now at 84 years old, he is still a working man. My grandpa never had a hobby. Working was and is his hobby. He does not fish, he does not golf, he does not have classic cars or trucks. Growing up, it seemed to me like Grandpa was always outside working. Now, he did have seven children (6 girls and 1 boy), so maybe that is why he was outside working all the time.

One day in the summer, when I was about 10 years old, my grandpa was baling hay on a hill on their farm by himself. When something was wrong with his baler, he would hop off the tractor, letting it putter very slowly down the hill while he fixed the baler. Then he would hop back on the moving tractor. He would later say the Holy Spirit told him to stop doing that, but he didn't listen.

Well, this day, when he went to hop back on the tractor, his foot slipped and he fell on his back with his legs underneath the tractor. The back tire of the tractor ran right over his midsection, and the baler was heading for him. He was so injured at that point he could not move. Balers have rakes that rake up the hay before it is put into bales. If those rakes had hit him, it most likely would have killed him. Grandpa, being a man of faith, cried out, "Jesus." He was in a troubled time and he didn't speak fear, he didn't speak unbelief and he didn't cuss. He used his words to accomplish something. The moment he cried out, "Jesus," something picked him up and threw him out of the way of the baler. He was protected by the supernatural power of God!

Grandpa was airlifted to a hospital and in pretty bad shape. After they stabilized him, one of the initial reports was that he may never walk again. One of the things I remember as a 10-year-old boy is that my grandma and grandpa would only say what the Word of God said about my grandpa being healed. As a little boy, I don't remember any fear in the house in regards to that situation. I do not remember ever hearing any unbelief. I heard words of faith and words of healing being spoken over my grandpa. Looking back on it now, I can tell you that there was an atmosphere of faith in the house. They had made the decision that they were only going to say what the Word of God says and nothing else. I never heard anything like, "Grandpa may never be the same again. Grandpa may never walk again. Grandpa might have to watch your ball games in a wheelchair." I heard things like, "God is going to heal Grandpa and he will walk again. The doctor said that, but God says this. Nothing is impossible with God." Seeing my grandma, my grandpa and others operate in faith in that situation left a mark of faith in my heart that will never be erased. I am happy to report to you, that my grandpa did walk again and is still walking today! Our God is a God of miracles!

After walking with the Lord for many years now and learning about the principles of faith and victory from the Word of God, I can see how vitally important it was that my grandma and grandpa did not let the enemy into their mouths. The words of faith that they spoke created an atmosphere of faith, and it was the breeding ground for this miracle. I am sure they were tempted at times to speak doubt and unbelief. However, they made the decision that they were not going to let the enemy into their mouths! They were going to say what the Word said and nothing else!

We must be on guard against speaking the wrong words, particularly in times of pressure. When you are under pressure, that is when you are the most susceptible to say the wrong thing. When the squeeze is being put on you, when things aren't changing, or when the situation looks like it's getting worse, you will be tempted to say the wrong thing.

One of the biggest challenges that you will face in a trying time is the challenge of not allowing your circumstances to dictate your speech. You will face trying times. You will have negative thoughts come to you. You will experience negative emotions. There will be times where it looks like your situation is not changing. You must not allow your circumstances to dictate your speech. You have to determine in your heart that you are only going to say what the Word of God says and nothing else!

SATAN HAS TO GET GOD'S WORDS OUT OF YOUR MOUTH

Once you have determined to say only what the Word of God says, the enemy will always come and try to get you to say something else.

In Daniel 3, King Nebuchadnezzar built an idol and commanded the people in the land to bow to that idol when the sound of music was played. Shadrach, Meshach and Abednego were three godly men who would not bow down because they had a commandment from God not to worship any other gods. Nebuchadnezzar had them brought into his quarters and told them that he was going to play the music one more time, and if they did not bow, they were going to be thrown into the fiery furnace. Daniel 3:16 says,

Shadrach, Meshach, and Abednego answered and said to the king, "O Nebuchadnezzar, we have no need to answer you in this matter. If it be so, our God whom we serve is able to deliver us from the burning fiery furnace, and He will deliver us from your hand, O king. But if not, let it be known to you, O king, that we do not serve your gods, nor will we worship the gold image which you have set up."

Satan knows that with these words in their mouths, he cannot have victory in their lives. Consequently, he has to do something to get them to say something different. What does he do? He increased the pressure. Verse 19 says, "Then was Nebuchadnezzar full of fury, and the form of his visage was changed against Shadrach, Meshach, and Abednego: therefore he spake, and commanded that they should heat the furnace one seven times more than it was wont to be heated." Fire itself is already hot, so why did he have the furnace heated up seven times hotter? This is an intimidation tactic of the enemy to get the Word of God out of their mouths. Satan was tightening the screws down on them in an attempt to get them to change what they were believing and saying.

They didn't give in to the enemy's attempt against their lives and in turn they experienced a great victory. Verses 23-28 say,

And these three men, Shadrach, Meshach, and Abed-Nego, fell down bound into the midst of the burning fiery furnace. Then King Nebuchadnezzar was astonished; and he rose in haste and spoke, saying to his counselors, "Did we not cast three men bound into the midst of the fire?" They answered and said to the king, "True, O king." "Look!" he answered, "I see four men loose, walking in the midst of the fire; and they are not hurt, and the form of the fourth is like the Son of God." Then Nebuchadnezzar went near the mouth of the burning fiery furnace and spoke, saying, "Shadrach, Meshach, and Abed-Nego, servants of the Most High God, come out, and come here." Then Shadrach, Meshach, and Abed-Nego came from the midst of the fire. And the satraps, administrators, governors, and the king's counselors gathered together, and they saw these men on whose bodies the fire had no power; the hair of their head was not singed nor were their garments affected, and the smell of fire was not on them. Nebuchadnezzar spoke, saying, "Blessed be the God of Shadrach, Meshach, and Abed-Nego, who sent His Angel and delivered His servants who trusted in Him, and they have frustrated the king's word, and yielded their bodies, that they should not serve nor worship any god except their own God!"

The moment God's Word gets in your heart and mouth, the enemy comes to try to get it out of your heart and mouth. In Mark 4:15, Jesus said, "Satan comes immediately, and takes away the Word that was sown in their hearts." This is what he tried to do with the three Hebrews, but he was unsuccessful. He could not get God's Words out of their mouths.

In 1 Samuel 17, David had been sent down to the battle by his father to bring supplies and to get an update on how things were going. The moment David stepped on the scene, Goliath appeared. 1 Samuel 17:23-24 says,

And as David talked with them, behold, there came up the champion, the Philistine of Gath, Goliath by name, out of the armies of the Philistines, and spake according to the same words: and David heard them. And all the men of Israel, when they saw the man, fled from him, and were sore afraid.

It's no coincidence that the moment David steps on the scene, out comes Goliath to try to put fear in him. Satan perceived that there was someone on the scene who was a threat to his plan in this situation. Satan knew there was somebody on the scene with enough faith in God to thwart his attempt against God's people. Verse 25 says, "And the men of Israel said, 'Have ye seen this man that is come up? surely to defy Israel is he come up: and it shall be, that the man who killeth him, the king will enrich him with great riches, and will give him his daughter, and make his father's house free in Israel.'" These men were trying to get David to be afraid with them. They wanted David to be impressed by this "great warrior," but he was not. It is important to be mindful of who you are spending time with because sometimes well-meaning Christians will try to get you to jump into unbelief with them. When you are in a dark place, you don't need to be hanging around people like this. In verse 26, we find David's declaration of faith. It says, "And David spake to the men that stood by him, saying, 'What shall be done to the man that killeth this Philistine, and taketh away the reproach from Israel? for who is this uncircumcised Philistine, that he should defy the armies of the living God?'" You can tell from these words that David is not only talking about fighting this giant, but he is talking about defeating him. Satan hates these words and knows he can't get victory over David with these words in David's mouth.

So, the enemy tried to tighten the screws down on David, and he used David's brother Eliab to do it. Verse 28 says,

And Eliab his eldest brother heard when he spake unto the men; and Eliab's anger was kindled against David, and he said, "Why camest thou down hither? and with whom hast thou left those few sheep in the wilderness? I know thy pride, and the naughtiness of thine heart; for thou art come down that thou mightest see the battle."

What is Satan doing through Eliab? He's trying to shut David up and get those words out of David's mouth. That was the first attempt the enemy made to get the Word out of David's mouth.

David turned around and asked the people again, "What does the guy get who kills this Philistine?" So, they sent David into Saul's tent, and in verse 32, we hear David's confession of faith. It says, "And David said to Saul, 'Let no man's heart fail because of him; thy servant will go and fight with this Philistine.'" Once again, Satan knows he cannot win with these words in David's mouth, so what does he do? He tries to tighten the screws down on David again, and this time he uses King Saul to do it. Verse 33 says, "And Saul said to David, 'Thou art not able to go against this Philistine to fight with him: for thou art but a youth, and he a man of war from his youth.'" Saul was an expert warrior himself and had won many battles. David has an "expert" telling him he can't do it. Sometimes the enemy will use so-called "experts" to try to get God's Word out of your mouth. However, this didn't change David's confession. Verses 34-37 say,

And David said unto Saul, "Thy servant kept his father's sheep, and there came a lion, and a bear, and took a lamb out of the flock: And I went out after him, and smote him, and delivered it out of his mouth: and when he arose against me, I caught him by his beard, and smote him, and slew him. Thy servant slew both the lion and the bear: and this uncircumcised Philistine shall be as one of them, seeing he hath defied the armies of the living God." David said moreover, "The LORD that delivered me out of the paw of the lion, and out of the paw of the bear, he will deliver me out of the hand of this Philistine." And Saul said unto David, "Go, and the LORD be with thee."

Satan is trying to get David to stop talking words of faith, but for the second time in a row, Satan failed.

The enemy tries one more time to get these words out of David's mouth, and this time he uses Goliath. Verses 41-44 say,

And the Philistine came on and drew near unto David; and the man that bare the shield went before him. And when the Philistine looked about, and saw David, he disdained him: for he was but a youth, and ruddy, and of a fair countenance. And the Philistine said unto David, "Am I a dog, that thou comest to me with staves?" And the Philistine cursed David by his gods. And the Philistine said to David, "Come to me, and I will give thy flesh unto the fowls of the air, and to the beasts of the field."

Why would Goliath speak these words? These words are the inspired utterance of the evil one. They were Satan's final attempt to get David to say something else. Verses 45–51 say,

Then said David to the Philistine, "Thou comest to me with a sword, and with a spear, and with a shield: but I come to thee in the name of the LORD of hosts, the God of the armies of Israel, whom thou hast defied. This day will the LORD deliver thee into mine hand; and I will smite thee, and take thine head from thee; and I will give the carcasses of the host of the Philistines this day unto the fowls of the air, and to the wild beasts of the earth; that all the earth may know that there is a God in Israel. And all this assembly shall know that the LORD saveth not with sword and spear: for the battle is the LORD'S, and he will give you into our hands." And it came to pass, when the Philistine arose, and came, and drew nigh to meet David, that David hastened, and ran toward the army to meet the Philistine. And David put his hand in his bag, and took thence a stone, and slang it, and smote the Philistine in his forehead, that the stone sunk into his forehead; and he fell upon his face to the earth. So David prevailed over the Philistine with a sling and with a stone, and smote the

Philistine, and slew him; but there was no sword in the hand of David. Therefore David ran, and stood upon the Philistine, and took his sword, and drew it out of the sheath thereof, and slew him, and cut off his head therewith. And when the Philistines saw their champion was dead, they fled.

The enemy could not get his words into David's mouth; therefore, he could not defeat him.

Satan can't stop a person who will keep talking faith in the midst of adversity. Often, we have made David's story about rocks, slingshots and armor. David's story is not about rocks, slingshots and armor, but rather it is about a man who would only speak God's words, no matter how great the pressure got.

You may be in the darkest place you've ever been, but if you'll keep the Word of God in your mouth and not allow the pressure to dictate your speech, you can overcome! The enemy will prod you, poke you and pressure you in an attempt to get control of your mouth. This is what he did with both David and the three Hebrews. If the pressure increases, just dig your feet in and hold fast to the confession of your faith. Winds may be blowing, circumstances may be getting worse, but you just keep believing and saying what God says. Your attitude must be one that says, "Satan, you cannot have my mouth! I'll never say what you want me to say! I'll die before I speak your words!" If you will make that your battle cry in the dark place, you will be delivered, you will triumph, and you will overcome!

FOUR STEPS TO PUTTING YOUR WORDS TO WORK

As we close out this chapter, I want to give you four practical steps to putting your words to work right in the middle of a trying time.

Step 1: Find Out What God Says

The first thing you must do is find out what the Word of God says about your situation. If you are battling sickness and disease, find out what God says in His Word about it. If you are facing a financial struggle, find out what God says in His Word about it. If you are battling anxiety and depression, find out what God says in His Word about it. Until you know what God says, you don't know what to say. Many believers do not have the first clue about what the Bible says about their situation. The problem is that religion does not teach us to run to the Word of God, but rather it teaches us to beg God to do something. If you do not know what God says about your situation, then how can you know what you should say about your situation?

Jesus operated in such a way where He only said what the Father said. In John 8:26–28, Jesus said, "I have many things to say and to judge of you: but he that sent me is true; and I speak to the world those things which I have heard of him. I do nothing of myself; but as my Father hath taught me, I speak these things." Jesus found out what the Father wanted Him to say and that is what He said. In John 12:49–50, Jesus said, "For I have not spoken of myself; but the Father which sent me, he gave me a commandment, what I should say, and what I should speak. And I know that his commandment is life everlasting; whatsoever I speak therefore, even as the Father said unto me, so I speak." You can see again in this verse that Jesus said what the Father said. John 3:34 says, "For he whom God hath sent speaks the Words of God."

When facing a trying situation, the first thing you must do is go to the Word of God and discover what God has to say about your situation. This is not something you should rush. Take your time and go through God's Word and find multiple scriptures concerning your situation. Before you speak, you have to take the time to discover what you should say.

Step 2: Choose To Believe What God Says

The second thing we must do in putting our words to work is to choose to believe what God has said to us in His Word, in regards to our situation. If you do not believe what God says, you will not say what He says. 2 Corinthians 4:13 says, "I have believed therefore have I spoke." The believing comes before the speaking, and if you don't choose to believe what God says, you won't say what He says. Therefore, it is imperative that you go to the Word of God, find out what God says about your situation, and then choose to believe it.

For example, if you are battling sickness and disease, you have to choose to believe what God says to you in His Word about it. You have to choose to believe that the God you serve is the Lord who heals you (Exodus 15:26). You have to choose to believe that the God you serve will heal all your diseases (Psalm 103:3). You have to choose to believe that the God you serve will take sickness away from the midst of you (Exodus 23:25). You have to choose to believe that Jesus took your infirmities and bore your sicknesses (Matthew 8:16). You have to choose to believe that as a seed of Abraham, healing belongs to you (Galatians 3:29, Luke 13:18). You have to choose to believe that by Jesus' stripes you are healed (Isaiah 53:5, 1 Peter 2:24).

Faith is a choice. You believe what you believe because you chose to believe. Whatever you do not believe right now is because you have not made the choice to believe. Again, faith is a choice.

Faith is not automatic. You do not believe God's Word automatically because you are a Christian. You do not believe God's Word automatically because you go to church. You do not believe God's Word automatically because you have read the Bible. If you haven't chosen to believe what God says about your situation, then you don't believe what God has said about your situation. Psalm 91:2 says, "I will say of the Lord, He is my refuge and my fortress: my God; in him will I trust." The psalmist chose to believe. He chose to trust. In Isaiah 7:9, the Lord said to His people, "If you will not believe, you surely will not be established." The use of the word will in these verses indicates that belief is a choice. Often times you will hear people say, "I just can't believe that." That is a lie. Faith is a choice, and you can believe whatever you choose to believe. What people should say instead of, "I just can't believe that," is, "I just won't believe that." Use of the word can't indicates that you don't have the ability to believe. Use of the word won't indicates you do have the ability to believe, but you are choosing not to.

Faith is a spiritual force, and it has to be turned on or activated, otherwise it will not work. You activate your faith with your will and with your words. Psalm 56:3 says, "What time I am afraid, I will trust in you." Psalm 61:3-4 says, "For you have been a shelter for me, and a strong tower from the enemy. I will abide in thy tabernacle forever: I will trust in the covert of your wings." When you say, "I choose to believe that," and mean business when you say it, you just activated your faith. Until you exercise your will and use your words where your faith is concerned, faith lays dormant. We have to believe on purpose. We don't believe just because we want to or just because we know we should. We don't believe until we choose to believe. For so many, their faith lays dormant because they never choose to believe.

I'VE HEARD THAT VERSE 1,000 TIMES

When I had been in ministry for about 12 years, I had concerns about the future of my ministry. Things were not progressing as fast as I would have liked. I had gotten to the place where I had taken the care of the future of my ministry and it pushed me into a state of concern. I let fear and unbelief get the best of me in this area. I had allowed this heaviness to sit upon me about the future of my ministry.

I was in my office one day, in a time of prayer. I had allowed the care of my ministry to just kind of hover over me. I was walking around my office praying, and a picture I had on my wall caught my attention. It was a picture that said, "Be Brave." The accompanying scripture was Jeremiah 29:11: "For I know the plans I have for you declares the Lord, plans to prosper you and not to harm, plans to give you hope and a future."

I first read that verse on a bulletin board at Lewis & Clark Community College, in Godfrey, Illinois, in 2001, when I was a freshman there. That verse was printed out on a colorful piece of paper and it caught my attention. I had just started reading my Bible on a regular basis, so when I saw that verse, it excited me. From the first time I saw that verse at Lewis and Clark Community College, to the day I was praying in my office, I had probably read that verse at least 500 times in my life. I had heard that verse preached on multiple times. I had preached on that verse myself multiple times. Needless to say, when that picture on the wall caught my attention, it was not the first time I had ever seen that verse.

However, this time when I read it, the Lord said to me, "Choose to believe that." I did just that. I said out loud, "I choose to believe that." I began to just declare that verse and meditate on that verse and began to say repeatedly, "I choose to believe that verse. I choose to believe God has a good plan for my life. I choose to believe the future of this ministry is bright." When I exercised my will and used my words like that, I activated my faith. The joy of the Lord came all over me, and I was no longer worried about my future. I was swimming in the peace of God!

That verse was doing nothing for me in my life until I activated my faith by choosing to believe it. Five minutes before this happened, if you would have asked me if I believed that verse, I would have said yes. However, there is a difference between mentally acknowledging that something is true and actually activating your faith and believing it. Prior to choosing to believe that verse, I was in a place where I would have mentally acknowledged it was true, but my faith was not turned on because I had not chosen to believe it.

MIX IT WITH FAITH

You must mix the Word of God with faith. Otherwise, the Word will not benefit you in your life. Hebrews 4:2 says, "For unto us was the gospel preached as well as unto them: but the Word preached did not profit them, not being mixed with faith in that that heard it." The profit is in the mixture, and until you mix the Word of God with your own faith, it will never profit you. Hearing the Word alone will not make the Word work for you. Knowing what the Word says alone, will not cause the Word to work for you. You have to choose to believe the Word. Then, and only then, will you see the Word profit you in your life.

This concept of choosing to believe may seem elementary, but it most certainly is not something to rush past. If you are in the midst of a troubled time, you need to take the time in prayer to go to each verse the Lord has led you to in regards to your situation, and you need to stop at each verse and activate your faith. Read the verse out loud and then stop and say, "I choose to believe that." Then go to the next verse and do the same thing. Read that verse out loud and then stop and say, "I choose to believe that." This is a life-changing practice!

Step 3: Choose What You Will Say

The third step in putting your words to work is that you must

95

choose what you will say. You choose your words. Psalm 91:2 says, "I will say of the Lord, He is my refuge and my fortress." Numbers 24:13 says, "What the Lord saith, that will I speak." We can see from these verses that we choose our words. If you said something, it is because you chose to say it. What you say is your choice.

Even Jesus had to choose His words. In John 8:26, He said, "I have many things to say and to judge of you: but he that sent me is true; and I speak to the world those things which I have heard of him." You don't automatically say what God says because you are a Christian. You don't automatically say what God says because you go to church or read your Bible. If you do say what God says, it will be because you chose to do so.

In times of pressure, there are many different things you can choose to say. You can choose to talk the problem. You can choose to talk your circumstances. You can choose to talk your feelings. Or, you can choose to say what God says.

In Numbers 13, when the 12 spies came back from spying out the land, ten of them chose to speak the problem, while the other two chose to say what God said. Numbers 13:25–32 says,

And they returned from searching of the land after forty days. And they went and came to Moses, and to Aaron, and to all the congregation of the children of Israel, unto the wilderness of Paran, to Kadesh; and brought back word unto them, and unto all the congregation, and showed them the fruit of the land. And they told him, and said, "We came unto the land whither thou sentest us, and surely it floweth with milk and honey; and this is the fruit of it. Nevertheless the people be strong that dwell in the land, and the cities are walled, and very great: and moreover we saw the children of Anak there. The Amalekites dwell in the land of the south: and the Hittites, and the Jebusites, and the Amorites, dwell in the mountains: and the Canaanites dwell by the sea, and by the coast of Jordan. We be not able to go up against the people; for they are stronger than we. The land, through which we have gone to search it, is a land that eats up the inhabitants thereof; and all the people that we saw in it are men of a great stature."

You have one group of people talking the problem, talking what they saw and talking what they felt. They are talking about the giants and the walls. They are talking about how they feel like grasshoppers. Those are the words they chose to speak. Joshua and Caleb chose to say what God said.

In troubled times, you will have to choose what words you will speak. That decision will confront you in the midst of every troubling situation that you encounter. This question rings loud in the realm of the spirit: "What words will they speak?" You can choose to talk the problem. You can choose to talk your feelings. You can choose to talk what you see. Or, you can choose to talk the Word. You can choose to say what God says. It is a choice that you will have to make.

The words you choose to speak in troubled times will have everything to do with whether or not you experience victory in troubled times. The simple reality is that if you do not get it right where your words are concerned, things are not going to go well for you. Proverbs 18:20–21 (Century English Version) says, "Make your words good – you will be glad you did. You will eat everything you say." We need to choose our words carefully. We particularly need to do so in troubled times. What will you say when you don't see? What will you say when you don't feel? What will you say when it looks like victory is impossible? What will you say when it looks like things are getting worse? So often, in so many situations, this is where the battle is won or lost.

Step 4: Believe That What You Say Will Come To Pass

The fourth step in putting your words to work is to believe that what you say will come to pass. Mark 11:22–23 says,

Jesus answering saith unto them, "Have faith in God. For verily I say unto you, That whosoever shall say unto this mountain, Be thou removed, and be thou cast into the sea; and shall not doubt in his heart, but shall <u>believe that those things which he saith shall come to pass</u>; he shall have whatsoever he saith."

If you want to put your words to work and see them work, then you have to believe that what YOU say will come to pass. The word believe in that verse means to be convinced or persuaded. To see your words work in a troubled time, you have to be convinced that what you say will come to pass.

Many speak God's Word and want it to come to pass or hope it comes to pass, but they are not convinced that what they say will come to pass. When God said, "Let there be light," He had no doubt His Words would come to pass. When Jesus spoke to the storm and said, "Peace, be still," He was convinced that what He said would come to pass. When David spoke to Goliath, he was convinced that what he said would come to pass. To put our words to work in troubled times and see them work, we have to be convinced that what we say will come to pass.

Step 5: Hold Fast To The Confession Of Your Faith

The fifth and final step in seeing your words work is to hold fast to the confession of your faith. That means you do not let go of what you are saying. You do not change what you are saying. Hebrews 10:23 says, "Let us hold fast the profession of our faith without wavering."

Once you discover what God has to say about your situation, that is what you say, and come hell or high water, you do not change. In Mark 5:28 (Amplified Bible) it says the woman with the issue of blood kept saying, "If I may but touch his clothes, I shall be whole." She kept saying it. She held fast to the confession of her faith. If you are going to experience victory in troubled times, you will have to do the same thing.

In times of great pressure, what we say is a vital component in experiencing victory. It is nearly impossible to overstate the significance of your words when you are facing a trying situation. Let me encourage you one final time as we close out this chapter: discover what God has to say about your situation and then get your mouth in gear by saying only what He says!

CHAPTER 4

DON'T BE EMOTIONAL, BE TACTICAL

When you are under attack or facing a troubled time, your emotions try to run wild. In times of pressure, you will experience a wide range of emotions. You will experience feelings of fear, sorrow and anger. These feelings tend to increase in intensity in a high-pressure situation or when facing a troubled time. You need to know that in a troubled time, it is completely normal to experience an array of emotions.

The emotions themselves are not the problem. Having negative feelings or experiencing negative emotions is not the problem. The problem is when we allow these emotions to dictate what we do. God warns us about this in His Word. Ephesians 4:26 says, "Be angry and sin not." The word angry in this verse means any violent emotion. It means to be exasperated, irritated, enraged. It also deals with the agitation of the soul.

Now, you will notice God did not tell us to not feel angry.

Rather, He said, "Be angry and sin not." In the same way, God never told us not to feel sad, anxious or afraid. It is a normal part of the human existence to experience all these emotions. Jesus experienced a wide range of emotions in His earthly life and ministry. You should never feel bad because you are experiencing some negative emotions. You should never feel bad for feeling bad.

God is instructing us in Ephesians 4:26 to not allow our emotions to move us in a direction that is in opposition to Him or in opposition to His Word. Let's read that verse one more time. It says, "Be angry and sin not." When you or I sin, we are moving in a direction that is in opposition to God and to His Word. When we sin, we are believing, talking or acting in a way that disagrees with God and His Word. If we are experiencing negative emotions, and we allow those emotions to move us in a direction that is in opposition to God and to His Word, that puts us in the wrong. That's what God is telling us not to do. We are commanded by God to not allow our emotions to move us into sin. You can see clearly that having a negative emotion is not the problem. Allowing that negative emotion to dictate what you do is the problem. It is okay to have feelings, it's not okay to follow your feelings.

This issue is paramount if you want to experience victory in troubled times. In a troubled time, you will have a wide-ranging array of emotions. If you want to triumph and overcome, then you must not allow the emotions you are having to dictate what you do.

MY FEELINGS ARE NOT MY GOD

As believers, we are supposed to be led by the Holy Spirit. Romans 8:14 says, "For as many as are led by the Spirit of God, they are the sons of God." Sons of God are supposed to be led by the Spirit of God. What you'll find in life is that what the Spirit of God is leading you to do, and what you feel like doing, so often are complete opposites. When your feelings are pulling you one way and the Spirit of God is leading you another way, you are supposed to follow the Holy Spirit and not your feelings. If you are following negative emotions, then you are not following the Holy Spirit.

Allowing your emotions to dictate what you do, or following your feelings, is one of the most dangerous things you can do in your life. Philippians 3:19 says, "Whose end is destruction, whose God is their belly." One meaning of the word belly is feelings. God's Word Translation says, "Their own emotions are their god." For your emotions to be your God, means you have submitted to your emotions. It means you are following your emotions. It means you are going to do what your emotions tell you to do.

It's important to note the kind of results you will experience if emotions are your god. Philippians 3:19 says, "Whose end is destruction." Following your feelings will lead to destruction in your life. This is why it is so vitally important, particularly in a troubled time, to not be moved by how you feel. Say this out loud, "My feelings are not my God." Say it again, "My feelings are not my God." One more time, "My feelings are not my God." What does that mean? That means you don't let your feelings rule your life. You don't let your emotions dictate what you do.

I DON'T FEEL LIKE DOING THAT

One thing that I have found in my life and ministry is that I rarely feel like doing what God wants me to do. My feelings do not always align with His commands. Years ago, God was prompting me to start our Faith For Life Broadcast, and I did not feel like doing that. Now, I thoroughly enjoy ministering the Word of God on the Faith For Life Broadcast. Not only that, but God is ministering to people in a great and mighty way through the broadcast. If I would have listened to my feelings, there would be no such thing as our Faith For Life Broadcast.

A few years ago, the Lord began dealing with me to launch Northsmoke Church. When it became clear to me that He wanted my wife Amber and me to do that, I did not feel like doing it. I was not sure I wanted to do that. I was hesitant and trepidatious — my feelings were not feeling it. I did not follow my feelings. We launched Northsmoke Church, and I enjoy pastoring the church as much as I have ever enjoyed anything in ministry. People are being ministered to through the church, and God is doing great things at Northsmoke Church. If I had listened to my feelings, none of that would be happening because I did not feel like starting the church.

In fact, you might find this funny, but I did not even feel like writing this book when I started. The opportunity to write this book came to me at a very busy time in my life. We were renovating the church at the time. I was recording The Faith For Life Broadcast every week. I was preaching every Sunday. My plate was full, and writing a book was one of the last things I felt like adding to my already full schedule. However, I sought the Lord and He dealt with me, convincing me that I needed to write this book. My feelings were not feeling it, but I stepped out by faith and started writing. As I began writing this book, I started to realize just how much I enjoyed ministering God's Word through writing. I also believe that this book is going to be a blessing to many people. If I had followed my feelings, you would not be reading this book right now.

As a believer, if you want to live in victory, you better get used to doing things that you do not feel like doing. You have to learn to follow God with or without the feelings. It begins with little things like going to church when you don't feel like it. Spending time in prayer when you don't feel like it. Reading your Bible when you don't feel like it. As you do these things, you'll develop the habit of being led by the Spirit instead of by your feelings.

If you want to experience victory in troubled times, you cannot allow your feelings to control you. When you are under pressure, there will be times when you feel like quitting and giving up. There will be times when you feel discouraged. There will be times when you feel afraid. There will be times when you feel like you can't go on. The only way to victory is through! You have to stay in faith, keep walking by faith, and you have to do that with those negative emotions all over you. If you bow your knee to those negative emotions and follow them, they will lead you into a place of defeat.

GOD WILL LEAD YOU INTO A GOOD PLACE

All throughout scripture, our God shows Himself to be a God who leads His people into good places. It started in Genesis when He created Adam and Eve and put them in a good place. The Garden of Eden was a good place. In Genesis 12:1–2, God told Abraham, "Now the Lord had said unto Abram, Get thee out of thy country, and from thy kindred, and from thy father's house, unto a land that I will shew thee: And I will make of thee a great nation, and I will bless thee, and make thy name great; and thou shalt be a blessing." God was leading Abraham into a good place. In the book of Exodus, God was endeavoring to lead the Children of Israel into the Promised Land. Ezekiel 20:6 calls the Promised Land, "The glory of all lands." It was a good place. Our God is a God who wants to lead His people into a good place. In fact, Psalm 23 is written about the good place our Good Shepherd wants to lead His people into. It says,

The Lord is my shepherd; I shall not want. 2 He maketh me to lie down in green pastures: he leadeth me beside the still waters. 3 He restoreth my soul: he leadeth me in the paths of righteousness for his name's sake. 4 Yea, though I walk through the valley of the shadow of death, I will fear no evil: for thou art with me; thy rod and thy staff they comfort me. 5 Thou preparest a table before me in the presence of mine enemies: thou anointest my head with oil; my cup runneth over. 6 Surely goodness and mercy shall follow me all the days of my life: and I will dwell in the house of the Lord forever.

The way to prosper, to be protected and to end up in a good place is to follow the Lord. To follow the Lord, you must not follow your feelings. Your feelings will actually lead you away from the good place that the Lord has for you.

Following negative emotions that are leading you in the opposite direction that the Lord is leading you is one of the most dangerous things you can do. The more you follow your feelings, the less you follow the Holy Spirit and the more trouble you will have.

A LIFE-CHANGING REALITY

Believe me friend, I understand that the feelings we have can be very strong. However, as believers we do not have to follow our feelings. Ephesians 4:26 says, "Be angry and sin not." That scripture leads us into this life-changing reality: We can have an emotion (feeling) and not be governed by it. Just because we feel angry does not mean we have to act on that anger and fly off the handle. We have been empowered by God to have an emotion and not be governed by it.

We are not at the mercy of our feelings. We are not slaves to our emotions. We can feel like saying something negative and not say it. We can feel like telling somebody off and not do it. We can feel like not going to church and go anyway. We can feel like not praising God and praise Him anyway. It is a powerful thing to realize that you don't have to act how you feel. You can feel one way and act another. You don't have to be ruled by your feelings.

One of the most powerful examples you will ever find in regards to not being at the mercy of your feelings is found in 1 Samuel 30. It says, starting in verse 1:

And it came to pass, when David and his men were come to Ziklag on the third day, that the Amalekites had invaded the south, and Ziklag, and smitten Ziklag, and burned it with fire; 2 And had taken the women captives, that were therein: they slew not any, either great or small, but carried them away, and went on their way. 3 So David and his men came to the city, and, behold, it was burned with fire; and their wives, and their sons, and their daughters, were taken captives. 4 Then David and the people that were with him lifted up their voice and wept, until they had no more power to weep. 5 And David's two wives were taken captives, Ahinoam the Jezreelitess, and Abigail the wife of Nabal the Carmelite. 6 And David was greatly distressed; for the people spake of stoning him, because the soul of all the people was grieved, every man for his sons and for his daughters: but David encouraged himself in the Lord his God.

David and his men had returned from battle and found their homes burned, their families taken captive and their possessions plundered. This falls under the category of a troubled time.

It's clear that David was experiencing negative emotions because the scripture says that he wept until he had no more power to weep. Verse 6 tells us that David was greatly distressed. Without question, David is in a troubled time, and he is experiencing a wide range of negative emotions.

In this troubled time, will David allow his emotions to dictate what he does? This is the big question that looms over David. The answer to this question will determine victory or defeat in this situation. If he allows his emotions to overtake him and acts emotionally, he will experience defeat. If he refuses to be governed by how he feels, seeks God and does what God says, then he will experience a great victory.

When we are facing troubled times, the same question lies before us. "Will we allow our emotions to dictate what we do?" Battles are won and lost right here at the feet of this question. We are all similar in that we will all experience troubled times, and we will all experience negative emotions in those troubled times. What separates the winners from the losers is the decisions we make when we are experiencing those negative emotions. David made the decision to not follow his feelings.

David was weeping and greatly distressed, but verse 6 tells us that he encouraged himself in the Lord. He felt discouraged, angry and maybe even afraid, yet he didn't allow those emotions to govern his life. He was not at the mercy of how he felt. He felt one way, but acted another. We don't have to act how we feel. We don't have to allow our emotions to dictate what we do. We don't have to follow our feelings. Our feelings are not our God. We can feel sad and choose to rejoice and be glad. We can feel afraid and choose to trust God and rest in His peace. We can feel like quitting and press on instead. David did not follow his feelings. Although he felt sad, angry and afraid, he didn't just sit there and wallow in his negative emotions.

Verse 8 says, "And David enquired at the Lord, saying, 'Shall I pursue after this troop? shall I overtake them?' And he answered him, 'Pursue: for thou shalt surely overtake them, and without fail recover all.'" David sought the Lord about what to do, and rather than following his feelings, David followed the Lord. As a result, he overtook the enemy and recovered all that they had stolen from him.

At the core of his victory was his decision to not allow his feelings to govern his life. After that battle, he returned home and found his family taken captive, his home burnt and his possessions plundered. With negative emotions all over him, he was at a crossroads. What will he do? Will he follow his feelings? Or will he follow the Lord?

In a troubled time, you and I will come to this same crossroads. Those same questions will lie before you. You are under great attack, your situation looks hopeless and you feel discouraged, afraid and sorrowful. What will you do next? What will you do when you experience negative emotions (because you will)? Battles are won and lost in these moments right here.

BE STRONG

Jesus was perfect and yet He experienced negative emotions. Therefore, it is safe to say we too will experience negative emotions. Luke 22:44 says, "And being in an agony he prayed more earnestly: and his sweat was as it were great drops of blood falling down to the ground." This was shortly before Jesus was to be crucified. The word agony means severe mental struggles and emotions. It is clear that Jesus was experiencing some negative emotions. Hebrews 4:15 says, "For we have not a high priest which cannot be touched with the feelings of our infirmities; but was in all points tempted like as we are, yet without sin." Jesus is touched with the feelings of our infirmities because He has felt what we feel. Although Jesus experienced negative emotions, He was never governed by His emotions. He never allowed His emotions to move Him into sin. That is an awesome reality. He felt what we felt but never allowed what He felt to move Him into sin.

Spiritual development in fulfillment is us becoming more and more like Jesus. Jesus was always led by the Spirit and never governed by His emotions. Therefore, the more like Jesus we become, the less governed by our emotions we will be. The more developed and mature you are spiritually, the less governed by your emotions you will be. When our emotions are controlling us and dictating what we do, it is a sign of spiritual immaturity. This is a sign of a lack of spiritual development. Why? Because to be spiritually mature is to be like the Master, and to be like the Master is to not be governed by your feelings.

Strong/mature/wise believers have learned the art of controlling their emotions rather than being controlled by their emotions. Proverbs 29:11 (God's Word Translation) says, "A fool expresses all his emotions, but a wise person controls them."

We are to rule our emotions, not be ruled by them. Proverbs 16:32 says, "He that rules his spirit is better than he that takes a city." The word spirit in that verse means the seat of the emotions. Our feelings should not be ruling over us and dictating what we do.

Psalm 42 gives us a perfect picture of someone controlling their emotions instead of being controlled by their emotions. Verse 11 (The Voice Translation) says, "Why am I so overwrought? Why am I so disturbed? Why can't I just hope in God? Despite all my emotions, I will believe and praise the One who saves me." He felt disturbed, he felt stressed, and yet he didn't allow those emotions to control him. In spite of how he felt, he praised God!

It is weak, foolish and immature to be governed by your feelings. Having emotions is not being weak, but being governed by them is weak. Anybody can feel angry and fly off the handle. That's being weak, foolish and immature because that is allowing your emotions to dictate what you do. Strong people don't fly off the handle in anger but rather control their emotions. Anybody can feel a little discouraged, drop their head and be sad. That's being weak, foolish and immature because that is allowing your emotions to dictate what you do. It takes a strong person to rejoice in the middle of that discouragement. Anybody can feel afraid and panic. That is being weak, foolish and immature because that is allowing your emotions to dictate what you do. A strong person will trust God and not panic, right in the face of that fear.

GOD WILL SPEAK TO YOU IN A DRIVE-THRU

Years ago, I was in a drive-thru with my wife when we got some news that a friend of ours had been terribly mistreated by another individual. When a person hurts someone you love, the first thing your flesh wants to do is go hurt that person in some way. Well, that day upon hearing this news, I started to experience an array of emotions. I was angry, I was upset, and I was hurting for this friend of ours. I thought about calling the individual who hurt my friend on the phone and giving them a piece of my mind. I thought about writing them a scathing text message. I thought about just driving over to their house and telling them off to their face. In times like this, the emotions we experience are very real. I was upset, and I could feel very real anger rising up within me. In the middle of experiencing all these emotions, the Lord spoke something to my heart. I believe it to be one of the most powerful things He has ever said to me. The Lord spoke to my heart and said, "Don't be emotional, be tactical." He quickly revealed to me that there were things I could do that would actually help my friend. He also revealed to me there were things I could do that would make the situation worse and make things harder on my friend. To be emotional would have been to act on those emotions I was having. Had I done that, I would have done something that made the situation worse and even more difficult for my friend. To be tactical is to set those emotions aside and do something that actually helps the situation. Being tactical is acting in a manner that will get you closer to your answer. Acknowledge the Lord, be led by His Spirit and do what He shows you to do. This is being tactical. This will get you closer to your answer. Praying in faith is being tactical. Speaking the Word of God over my friend is being tactical. Standing in faith for my friend is being tactical. Doing these things will actually help get this situation closer to where we want it to be. Calling that person that hurt my friend and telling them off is just being emotional. Texting them and telling them off is just being emotional. Going to their house and telling them off to their face is just being emotional. None of that would have helped. None of that would have helped my friend.

Captain Roger Herbert was a former commander of the Navy Seal training program. He made a very interesting comment about the importance of a soldier controlling their emotions in battle. He said, "When you look at historic mistakes on the battlefield, they are almost always associated with fear and panic. So the capacity to control these impulses is extremely important." If a solider is governed by his emotions in a time of attack, he will act emotionally, make a mistake and be defeated. He must be tactical and not emotional in these high-pressure situations if he wants to come out on top.

In troubled times, emotions will run high, and if you act emotionally, you will make a mistake spiritually and be defeated. It is imperative, particularly in troubled times, that we keep our emotions in check. You will experience emotions and some will be very strong, but do not act emotionally. Do not be emotional, be tactical. Seek God, get into His Word and do what He shows you to do, no matter how you feel. This is being tactical.

REMEMBER YOUR TRAINING

Jesse Duplantis is a very well-known preacher whose ministry is out of New Orleans, Louisiana. He is someone the Lord has used in my life for many years. In fact, watching his messages on videotape in my late teens stirred a hunger in me to pursue my own relationship with the Lord. I am forever grateful for what the Lord did in my life through Jesse Duplantis.

Jesse is a traveling minister, so for many years he traveled a lot on commercial airlines. Years ago, he was on a commercial flight and the aircraft started to have some mechanical issues. I believe he said turbulence was bad and the oxygen masks had even fallen. Well, one of the stewardesses was getting emotional and panicking. Jesse grabbed her by the shoulders and shouted, "Hey, remember your training!" When he said that, she came out of that emotional state, remembered her training and the plane made it. She was allowing her emotions to get the best of her. Her emotional state was keeping her from doing the things she had been trained to do that would actually help in this situation.

Friend, what Jesse said to that stewardess works for us today. When you are under pressure and facing a troubled time, don't be emotional, remember your training. God has equipped and trained us through His Word about how we should operate in a time of pressure. There are things God has trained us to do that will actually help us enjoy victory in a troubled time. A lot of people, in a pressure situation, make the mistake of getting overly emotional and forgetting their training. They get emotional and do nothing that God trained them to do. No matter how dire the situation is, keep your emotions in check, remember your training and do what God has trained you to do!

BE SOBER

God speaks to these truths in 1 Peter 5:8. It says, "Be sober, be vigilant; because your adversary the devil, as a roaring lion, walketh about, seeking whom he may devour." The word sober means calm and collected in spirit. It means to be dispassionate or unmoved by feelings. God is instructing us to not allow our emotions to overtake us and govern us.

This verse starts off by telling us to be sober but then finishes up talking about our adversary looking for people he can devour. These two thoughts are connected.

If you get emotional and allow your emotions to dictate what you do, you are going to yield to the enemy and give him access into your life to devour you. He will try to work you into an emotional fit, to the place where you act emotionally, yield to him and give him access into your life. This is why God is telling us to be sober and to be unmoved by our feelings.

If we allow our emotions to dictate what we do, we are going to make a mistake, yield to the enemy and give him access into our lives. Therefore, we must be sober. We must be calm, collected, dispassionate and unmoved by our feelings. We will experience a multitude of different emotions, particularly in times of pressure, and that is a normal part of the human existence. However, we must not allow our emotions to overtake us and dictate what we do.

When God commanded us to be sober, He authorized us to do it and He empowered us to do it. Therefore, no matter how troubling the situation is that we are facing, we can be calm, cool, collected and unmoved by our feelings. We do not have to be governed by our feelings, no matter how intense the situation is. God has given to us the supernatural ability to be sober!

It is absolutely vital, when in a troubled time, to control your emotions and to be tactical. Proverbs 13:16 says, "Every prudent man deals with knowledge." Prudence means to foresee the consequences of an action. Prudence sees that if I do this, it will lead to that. If I get emotional and allow my emotions to dictate what I do, I'll let the enemy in, and I won't experience victory in this trying time. If

I control my emotions and look to God and look to His Word and do what He says, that will lead to my prosperity and success in this situation. The prudent man deals in knowledge, not in his emotions. Be prudent! Be tactical!

IT DOESN'T MATTER HOW I FEEL

When it comes to our emotions, one mistake that is easy to make is making too much of our feelings. Proverbs 29:11, in God's Word Translation says, "A fool expresses all his emotions." Why does a fool do that? Because to him, his feelings are a big deal, therefore, they are worthy of being expressed. A fool makes much of his feelings and focuses on his feelings.

In the grand scheme of things, our feelings really do not matter all that much. I don't mean that to be insensitive, but it is just true. What you believe matters. What you say matters. What you do matters. These things are the difference between experiencing victory or defeat, so they matter. How you feel, not so much.

Feelings are fickle. Feelings come and go. Feelings change. It is a big mistake to make too much of your feelings. The Lord gave me a statement years ago that I've used in my own life from time to time, and it's really helped me to not be governed by my feelings. Here it is: It doesn't matter how I feel. If you want to, say that out loud, "It doesn't matter how I feel." In a time of pressure, feelings can be running rampant. I am not minimizing the reality of that. The Lord is sensitive to that, and as believers, we should be sensitive to others who are emotional in a trying time. However, the fact of the matter is we have to trust God, hold onto His Word and have faith in Him in spite of our feelings. The great hall of fame basketball player Jerry West once said, "You can't get much done in life if you only work on the days you feel good." I would say you can't get very far spiritually if you only live by faith and obey God when you feel like it. We have to do what God says, say what He says and believe what He says no matter how we feel. These things actually matter, and they are the difference between winning and losing. When our feelings are going in every direction and trying to pull us out of faith, it would do us good to remind ourselves that it does not matter how we feel. If we want to experience victory in troubled times, we must not be moved by how we feel!

CHAPTER 5

I WILL

One of the most powerful things that you can do in a troubled time is exercise your will. Exercising your will in faith, in line with the Word of God, is extremely critical in experiencing victory in troubled times.

In the Bible, we see people in times of pressure exercise their will. We noted earlier how David wrote Psalm 23 in one of the most trying times of his life. In verse 4, he said, "Yea though I walk through the valley of the shadow of death, I will fear no evil." In the middle of this pressure situation, David exercised his will. He said, "I will not fear."

We see this again in Habakkuk 3:17-18. The writer said, "Although the fig tree shall not blossom, neither shall fruit be in the vines; the labor of the olive shall fail, and the fields shall yield no meat; the flock shall be cut off from the fold, and there shall be no herd in the stalls: 18 Yet I will rejoice in the Lord, I will joy in the God of my salvation." This is obviously a trying time that he is facing. It was a time of lack and scarcity. Right in the middle of that pressure situation, he exercised his will and said, "I will rejoice in the Lord, I will joy in the God of my salvation."

We see this same principle again in Psalm 3:6. It says, "I will not be afraid of ten thousands of people, that have set themselves against me round about." The psalmist is surrounded by his enemies. His chances of survival seem non-existent. In the middle of this trying time, he exercises his will and says, "I will not be afraid."

In Psalm 56:3-4 we see the same idea again. It says, "What time I am afraid, I will trust in you. In God I will praise his words. In God I have put my trust; I will not fear what flesh can do unto me." The psalmist again found himself facing daunting circumstances. Fear was obviously trying to come all over him. Yet, in this trying time, he exercised his will and said, "I will trust in you. I will praise God's words. I will not fear."

THANK GOD I LIVE IN THE COUNTRY

Earlier, I shared with you how in 2011 the enemy attacked me in many different areas of my life. One of the areas he attacked me the most was with fear. Now, anybody who has dealt with feelings of fear and anxiety knows that these feelings can be very strong and very real. However, that doesn't change the fact that we have authority over fear in the name of Jesus. Through the power of that name, and through the power of the Word of God, we can put fear and anxiety in the ground and experience victory in our lives.

One particular day, fear was attacking me in a pretty strong way. Up until this point, I hadn't gained much ground spiritually on this fear that I was dealing with. It seemed to be hovering over me on a daily basis. One day, I was in my office at home when this fear tried to come on me. I recognized it was the devil, so I grabbed my Bible and decided to walk our property and pray. I went outside and opened my Bible and began to speak God's Word over my life. After doing that for a few moments, my faith climaxed, and I shouted as loud as I could, "I will not fear!" Now, that's the kind of thing they will call the cops on you for if you live in town. We live out in the country so I was safe.

The Lord revealed to me that if I was going to enjoy victory over fear, I was going to have to exercise my will, right in the middle of the fear. I was going to have to exercise my will with feelings of fear all over me. I believe that to be a key moment in the battle that I was facing. It was a turning point. My victory was not instant, but it was not long after that, that I was completely delivered from that fear. I am convinced, that when I exercised my will, that whole situation shifted in my favor and towards my victory.

VICTORY REQUIRES SOMETHING OF US

You see, to live in victory, it requires something of us. Many like to pretend that we have no part to play in what God does or doesn't do in our lives. Many believe Jesus obtained the victory for us, so we just do nothing and wait for God to do something. Jesus did pay the price, the victory has been obtained, but that doesn't mean we don't have a part to play in our enjoying victory in our lives.

James 4:7 says, "Resist the devil and he will flee from you." God is talking to us in that verse. God doesn't resist the devil for us.

We must resist the devil if we want to see him flee from our lives. Resisting is our part. 1 Timothy 6:12 says, "Fight the good fight of faith." God was talking to us in that verse. He does not fight the good fight of faith for us. That's our part. Ephesians 6:11 says, "Put on the whole armor of God, that you may be able to stand against the wiles of the devil." God is talking to us in that verse. We have to put on His armor because we are the ones who have to fight and stand against the devil. God will help you do these things, but He will not do them for you. In Mark 11:22, Jesus said, "Have faith in God." God was talking to us in that verse. Our part is to believe, to trust and to have faith in God. That is a fight because the enemy doesn't want you in faith. God will not do that for you.

If we want to enjoy victory in troubled times, it is going to require something of us. If we sit back in a passive position spiritually, we will not enjoy victory in our lives. It is a nice thought to think we just sit back and do nothing and God does everything, but it's simply not true. Victory in the life of a believer requires something of the believer.

YOU CHOOSE

God gave to every person a will or the right to choose. We see this in the Garden of Eden in the beginning. In creation, God gave man a will. He told them to not eat of the tree, but He allowed them to choose for themselves. Deuteronomy 30:15-19 says,

See, I have set before thee this day life and good, and death and evil; 16 In that I command thee this day to love the Lord thy God, to walk in his ways, and to keep his commandments and his statutes and his judgments, that thou mayest live and multiply: and the Lord thy God shall bless thee in the land whither thou goest to possess it. 17 But if thine heart turn away, so that thou wilt not hear, but shalt be drawn away, and worship other gods, and serve them; 18 I denounce unto you this day, that ye shall surely perish, and that ye shall not prolong your days upon the land, whither thou passest over Jordan to go to possess it. 19 I call heaven and earth to record this day against you, that I have set before you, life and death, blessing and cursing: therefore choose life, that both thou and thy seed may live.

They could choose life and blessing by choosing to follow God, or they could choose death and the curse by choosing to turn away from God. It was their choice. They had a free will given to them by God, and it was their choice what they would do.

GOD WON'T MAKE YOU & THE DEVIL CAN'T MAKE YOU

God will never take your will from you and make you do something. God will let you do what you want to do even if it's not what He wants you to do. Psalm 81:11-13 says, "But my people did not listen to me. Israel did not obey me. 12 So I let them go their own stubborn way and do whatever they wanted. 13 If my people would listen to me and live the way I want, then I would defeat their enemies." God is not going to override your will and make you do the things necessary to enjoy victory in your life. You have to exercise your will and choose to do the things necessary to enjoy victory in troubled times.

God won't take your will from you, and the enemy can't take your will from you. One of our daughters, after she did something wrong one time, said from the backseat of the truck, "The devil made me do it." We quickly instructed her that the devil cannot make you do anything. He can try to inspire you to do something, but he can't make you do it.

I heard a preacher tell a story one time about a little girl and her brother. They were in the backseat of the car, and all of a sudden the little girl said out loud, "Shut up devil. Shut up devil." Her mom asked her, "Why did you say that?" The little girl said, "The devil told me to break my brother's leg." She had the right idea. The devil cannot override her will and make her do what he wants her to do. The same reality is true for us. The devil cannot make you get into unbelief. He cannot make you worry or fear. He cannot make you disobey God. God gave you your will, and the devil cannot take it from you. Your will is your will. You can choose whatever you desire to choose. You can say whatever you choose to say. You can think whatever you choose to think. You can believe whatever you choose to believe.

This has everything to do with experiencing victory in troubled times. To come out of that low place and into a place of victory, there are certain decisions you have to make. You have to choose to stay in faith. You have to choose to say what God says. You have to choose to do what God shows you to do. When you are under pressure, you won't always feel like staying in faith. When you're in a tight place, you won't always feel like saying what God says. When your situation looks hopeless, you won't always feel like doing what God shows you to do. This is where the power of exercising your will comes into play. You can exercise your will in troubled times and stay in faith when you don't feel like it. You can exercise your will in troubled times and say what God says when it looks like what He says will never come to pass. You can exercise your will in troubled times and do what God tells you to do, even when you feel like quitting. Decisions like these will propel you to victory!

ESTABLISH YOUR HEART

One big thing that happens when you exercise your will is that you establish your heart. Psalm 112:7-8 says, "He shall not be afraid of evil tidings: his heart is fixed, trusting in the Lord. His heart is established, he shall not be afraid." The word establish in that verse means to set firm or unchangeable. It also means to settle permanently. To establish your heart simply means that you are deciding and settling permanently what you are going to do. In this psalm, the psalmist established his heart that he would trust God and that he would not fear. How did he establish his heart concerning those things? He did it with a decision. He said, "I will trust. I will not be afraid."

When you exercise your will, you are settling permanently what you will do. When you exercise your will, you are starting something that you will not change or alter. When David said in Psalm 23:4, "I will not fear," he is establishing his heart. He is settling what he will do. He started something with that decision.

It is absolutely vital in a troubled time to exercise your will and establish your heart. In a trying time, the enemy will try to pull you a bunch of different directions. He will pull on you to get into unbelief. He will pull on you to speak his words. He will try to pull you into fear and sorrow. You have to establish your heart and settle what you are going to do. You do that by exercising your will. If you don't establish your heart by exercising your will, you will be inconsistent in all your ways. You will be up and you will be down. One day you will be in faith and the next you will be in unbelief. When you are under pressure, when the circumstances look daunting, and when defeat seems inevitable, you must establish your heart. Exercise your will and settle what you are going to do in the midst of the pressure.

You may be facing a daunting situation today. Maybe you are battling anxiety and depression. Maybe a loved one has died, and feelings of sorrow are all over you. What are you going to do? You can sit there and wallow in your feelings of anxiety and sorrow, or you can establish your heart in line with the Word of God. You can exercise your will and say, "I will cling to my good God. I will not fear. I will not fret. I will not sorrow. I will rejoice. I will be glad. I will overcome! I will triumph! I will win!" You might have to do that with tears rolling down your face, but decisions like these are where victory starts!

HOURS TO LIVE

Kellie Copeland has an awesome story about exercising her will and seeing a miracle. Kellie is Kenneth and Gloria Copeland's daughter. Years ago, when her daughter was just a little girl, she was hospitalized with meningitis. An outbreak had happened in their community, and many children were dying. Kellie took her daughter to the hospital, and the doctor came and told Kellie that her daughter only had hours to live.

Upon hearing that report, Kellie turned to her older sister, Terri, and said, "I will not fear." Kellie exercised her will and established her heart. At that moment, she settled what she was going to do. Kellie testified later that the moment she made that decision, the fear just lifted off of her.

A short time later, Kenneth and Gloria arrived at the hospital, and they went in to pray for their granddaughter. Brother Copeland went in there and ministered to his granddaughter, and the moment he said what the Lord told him to say to her, her eyes popped open, and she said, "Pawpaw, I'm healed!" This little girl was supernaturally healed by the power of God!

That victory started with her mom's established heart. With feelings of fear trying to come all over her, and with that death report staring her in the face, Kellie made a decision that produced a miracle in her daughter's life.

Trying times are just that, they are trying. They come with a wide range of thoughts and emotions that will try to pull you in a thousand different directions. If you don't exercise your will and settle what you're going to do, you don't stand a chance. You have to make the decision that you are going to have faith in God, come hell or high water, until victory shows up!

SET YOUR COURSE

Another big thing that happens when you exercise your will is you set your course. Decisions determine direction. Psalm 25:12 says, "What man is he that fears the Lord? Him shall he teach in the way that he shall choose." When you make a decision, you determine your direction. When you make a decision, you choose the way that you will go. That day when I went outside my house and declared, "I will not fear," I set my course. With that decision, I determined the direction I was going.

The direction you go determines the destination that you will reach. We live close to Interstate 55 in Illinois. A section of Interstate 55 runs from Saint Louis, Missouri, to Chicago, Illinois. If I get on Interstate 55 and choose to go southbound, in 30 minutes I'll be in Saint Louis. If I get on Interstate 55 and choose to go northbound, I will be in Chicago in four hours. My decision determines my direction, and the direction I go determines the destination that I will reach.

These things are true spiritually. Spiritually speaking, there is a way that leads to life, and there is a way that leads to death. Jeremiah 21:8 says, "Thus saith the Lord; Behold, I set before you the way of life and the way of death." There is a way you go spiritually that will lead to life and prosperity. There is a way you go spiritually that will lead to death and destruction. Whichever way you go will determine the destination you reach. The way you go is determined by the decision you make.

To end up at a victorious destination, you have to choose the way of faith and the way of the Word. If you choose to fear, to doubt and to yield to unbelief, that way will lead you to defeat. Don't go that way! In troubled times, when we exercise our will to trust God and go the way of His Word, we just set the course for our lives. When you go the way of trusting God, and when you go the way of His Word, it will always lead you to a victorious destination.

In troubled times, it is absolutely vital that you set your course by exercising your will. Until you make a decision and exercise your will, your course is not set. Herein lies the importance of exercising your will in troubled times. It sets your course in the midst of that troubled time. If you fail to exercise your will about the direction that you will go, you will stumble around in circles and never enjoy victory in your life. Decide which destination you want to reach, and then exercise your will to set your course towards that destination. To reach a victorious destination, we must choose the way of faith and the way of God's Word.

WE EXERCISE OUR WILL WITH OUR WORDS

The way we exercise our will is with our words. When you open your mouth and declare, "I will," you just exercised your will.

In scripture, we see people over and over again exercising their will with their words. In Psalm 23:4, David said, "Yea though I walk through the valley of the shadow of death, I will fear no evil." Psalm 118 says, "The Lord is on my side; I will not fear." Habakkuk 3:17–18 says,

Although the fig tree shall not blossom, neither shall fruit be in the vines; the labor of the olive shall fail, and the fields shall yield no meat; the flock shall be cut off from the fold, and there shall be no herd in the stalls: 18 Yet I will rejoice in the Lord, I will joy in the God of my salvation.

This is obviously a trying time that he is facing. It was a time of lack and scarcity. Right in the middle of that pressure situation he said, "I will rejoice in the Lord, I will joy in the God of my salvation." These decisions that they made were decrees. They used their words to exercise their will.

In a troubled time, you and I will have to do the same thing. In a troubled time, you should hear yourself exercising your will with your words. In fact, the phrase, "I will," should be a phrase you use frequently in a troubled time. You should hear yourself say, "I will have faith in God. I will trust Him. I will stand on His Word. I will say what He says! I will press on. I will continue on! I will stand strong! I will rejoice! I will be glad! I will not give into the enemy! I will not take that thought! I will not worry! I will not be anxious! I will not be sorrowful! I will not despair! I will not be afraid! I will not fear! I will not be defeated! I will fight! I will triumph! I will overcome! I will break through! I will win!" Exercising your will like this is one of the most powerful weapons we have in our arsenal. It is my personal opinion that we are not using this weapon nearly enough.

"I WILL" WHEN I DON'T SEE OR FEEL

One of the most powerful things you can do is exercise your will in line with the Word of God in spite of what you see and feel. In troubled times, we have to exercise our will, contrary to what we see and feel. When you feel afraid, you have to exercise your will and say, "I will not fear." When you don't feel like you have any faith at all, you have to exercise your will and say, "I will trust God." When you feel sad, discouraged and depressed, you have to exercise your will and say, "I will rejoice and be glad." When it looks like defeat is inevitable, you have to exercise your will and say, "I will triumph! I will win! I will overcome!" You have to choose to resist the enemy when it feels like he is bombarding you on every front. You have to choose to resist fear when it feels like fear is all over you. You have to choose to press on when you feel like quitting. When we make decisions in line with the Word of God, at the expense of our feelings, it positions us to experience great victories in our lives.

NOTHING BEGINS UNTIL SOMEBODY MAKES A DECISION

All turnarounds, breakthroughs and victories begin with a decision. Luke 15 tells the story of the prodigal son. He asked his father for his inheritance early, and then he proceeded to leave home and squander it all. He hit rock bottom. He wasted his inheritance and was eating with the pigs. He ended up coming back home; his father welcomed him back into the family, and all was well. Where did his turnaround begin? It began in Luke 15:18, when he said, "I will arise and go to my father, and will say unto him, Father, I have sinned against Heaven, and before you." His turnaround began with a decision.

David's victory over Goliath began with a decision. In 1 Samuel 17:32, David said, "And David said to Saul, 'Let no man's heart fail because of him; thy servant will go and fight with this Philistine.'" David said to Goliath in verse 46, "This day will the Lord deliver thee into mine hand; and I will smite thee, and take thine head from thee; and I will give the carcasses of the host of the Philistines this day unto the fowls of the air, and to the wild beasts of the earth; that all the earth may know that there is a God in Israel." David made a decision to go fight. David made a decision to go win.

Nothing begins until somebody makes a decision. My wife Amber and I dislike how indecisive we can be sometimes. Sometimes it will take us an hour to decide what we are going to eat for dinner. I am sure there are some other married couples that can relate to that. Here's the thing, nothing happens until we make a decision. This is true when you are in a trying time. In a trying time, you will not stumble upon victory accidently. Victory in troubled times comes as a result of making a series of conscious decisions that are in line with the Word of God. Where does your victory begin? It starts with a decision!

DECISIONS IN TROUBLED TIMES

The decisions we make in pressure times are the difference between winning and losing. In Luke 8, Jairus came to Jesus because his daughter was sick and about to die. Verses 41-42 say, "And, behold, there came a man named Jairus, and he was a ruler of the synagogue: and he fell down at Jesus' feet, and besought him that he would come into his house: For he had one only daughter, about twelve years of age, and she lay a dying." This is a time of great pressure for Jairus. This is a troubled time for him. Any parent knows how helpless it can feel when your child is sick. Without a doubt, Jairus is feeling some of these same things.

Verse 49 says, "There cometh one from the ruler of the synagogue's house, saying to him (Jairus), Thy daughter is dead; trouble not the master." Jairus' troubled time just got more troubling. He got a report from his house that his daughter was dead. This is a very intense, high-pressure situation. I am certain Jairus was experiencing all kinds of negative thoughts and emotions.

Verse 50 says, "But when Jesus heard it, he answered him saying, 'Fear not: believe only, and she will be made whole.'" When Jesus spoke these words, he laid the path of victory right before Jairus. If Jairus will fear not and believe only, his daughter will be made whole. All things, regarding this situation, hung in the balance awaiting Jairus' decision. He has a choice to make. He can choose to do what Jesus said. He can choose to fear not and to believe only, or he can choose to do the opposite. What happens in the life of his little girl is going to be based on the decision he makes.

There are high-leverage moments like this in every spiritual battle. Moments like these are where battles are won or lost. These kinds of moments put you at a crossroads and leave you with a choice to make. Friend, you will encounter these moments in your life. You will encounter these moments in troubled times. In moments like these, if you will exercise your will in faith and in line with the Word of God, you can't lose.

Jairus chose to do what the Master said. You talk about a man that lived by faith: they told him his daughter was dead, and he responded by choosing to fear not and believe only. In Luke 8:54-55 it says, "He [Jesus] took her by the hand, and called, saying, 'Maid, arise.' And her spirit came again, and she arose straightway." The decision Jairus made in a troubled time led to victory in his life!

OUR WORDS, OUR THOUGHTS, OUR BELIEFS

In experiencing victory in troubled times, there are three vital areas that you must exercise your will: what you say, what you think and what you believe. What you choose to say, what you choose to think on, and what you choose to believe are critical decisions in troubled times. There is a way of speaking, thinking and believing that leads to victory. There is also a way of speaking, thinking and believing that leads to defeat. In experiencing victory in troubled times, it is absolutely vital that you choose to say the right things, to think on the right things and to believe the right things. In troubled times, you must make a conscious decision about what you are going to say, what you are going to think and what you are going to believe. If you do not decide those things consciously and on purpose, you will end up talking in a way, thinking in a way and believing in a way that will lead to defeat. However, if you exercise your will in line with the Word of God, in regards to your words, thoughts and beliefs, it will position you to experience victory in troubled times.

In a time of pressure, you have to decide what you are going to say. In Psalm 91:2, the psalmist said, "I will say of the Lord, He is my refuge and my fortress." You can see from that verse that he made a conscious decision about what he was going to say. In times of pressure, you need to decide what you are going to say. You can choose to talk the problem, the circumstances and the evil report. Or, you can choose to say what the Word of God says. Often, people get in pressure situations and let their mouths go. They choose to speak words that lead to their defeat. In a pressure time, in a troubled time, you need to make a conscious decision about what you will say. How do you do that? You open up your mouth and say, "Regarding this situation, I will say only what the Word of God says."

In a time of pressure, you have to decide what you are going to think on. In a trying time, the mind comes under great attack. If you don't decide on purpose what you are going to think on, you will end up thinking on the wrong stuff. Psalm 119:48 says, "I will meditate in your precepts." The psalmist is deciding on purpose to think on God's Word. We need to be selective about what we think on because yielding to the wrong thought can lead to defeat. In Matthew 14, Peter took his eyes off of Jesus and chose to think about the wind and the waves, and it led to his defeat. In a trying time, you have to make a conscious decision about what you are going to think on. How do you do that? You open your mouth and say, "Regarding this situation, I will set my mind on what God's Word says, and I will not think on anything that contradicts His Word."

In a time of pressure, you have to decide what you are going to believe. Faith is a choice. What you believe is your choice. What you believe is vitally important when it comes to experiencing victory in troubled times. In troubled times, you need to open your mouth, exercise your will and declare, "I will trust God. I choose to have faith in Him. I choose to believe His Word."

THE RESPONSIBILITY OF CHOICE

In troubled times, the responsibility of choice falls on us. Joshua 24:15 says, "Choose you this day who you will serve." You can see clearly from that verse that the responsibility of choice falls on you. You have to choose who you are going to serve, follow and trust.

In Deuteronomy 30:19, God said, "I call heaven and earth to record this day against you, that I have set before you, life and death, blessing and cursing: therefore choose life, that both thou and thy seed may live." God had Heaven and Earth record the day against them because they were the ones responsible for the choice they made.

In a troubled time, you have to choose what you will believe, say and do. You have to choose whether or not you quit or press on. You have to choose whether or not you will be discouraged or rejoice. You have to choose whether or not you will resist the enemy or yield to him. The responsibility of choice falls on you. God will not make those choices for you.

The exciting reality is that when we make decisions in line with the Word of God, all of Heaven comes to our aid. When we align ourselves with God by making decisions in faith and in line with His Word, He will move on our behalf. When God moves on our behalf, the result will be victory in troubled times!

CHAPTER 6

KEEP YOUR HEART FULL OF THE WORD

The fifth and final key to victory in troubled times that we will discuss in this book is inarguably the most important one. To do the things necessary to experience victory in troubled times, you must keep your heart full of God's Word.

FILL YOUR HEART WITH HIS WORD

God told us repeatedly throughout scripture to keep our hearts full of His Word. Colossians 3:16 says, "Let the Word of Christ dwell in you richly." The word richly in that verse means abundantly. God's Words are supposed to be in us in abundance. In Deuteronomy 11:18–21, the Lord said,

Therefore shall you lay up these my words in your heart and in your soul, and bind them for a sign upon your hand, that they may be as frontlets between your eyes. And you shall teach them to your children, speaking of them when you sit in your house, and when you walk by the way, when you lie down, and when you rise up. And you shalt write them upon the door posts of thine house, and upon your gates, so that your days may be multiplied, and the days of your children in the land which the Lord swore unto your fathers to give them as the days of heaven upon the earth.

We are to lay up God's words in our hearts. The phrase lay up means to set, station or plant. God's Words are to be laid up, set, stationed and planted in our hearts. In Deuteronomy 6:6 (Contemporary English Version), God said, "These words that I am giving you today are to be in your heart." Proverbs 7:1–3 says, "My son, keep my words, and lay up my commandments with thee. Keep my commandments, and live; and my law as the apple of thine eye. Bind them upon thy fingers, write them upon the table of thine heart." Proverbs 4:20-21 says, "My son, attend to my words; incline thine ear unto my sayings. 21 Let them not depart from thine eyes; keep them in the midst of thine heart." God's Words are supposed to be in our hearts. God's Words are supposed to be written upon our hearts. God's Words are supposed to be kept in our hearts. The Word of God is supposed to take up residence in the heart of the believer. Believers are to be full of the Word of God all of the time!

We just looked at five references of God telling us to fill our hearts with His Word. There are more references of this throughout the Bible as well. If God says something one time, it should be important to us. However, when God says something to us again and again, it should take on an even higher level of significance and meaning. The reason that God repeats Himself regarding an issue is because that issue is very important. This issue of having your heart full of God's Word is of the utmost importance when you're talking about experiencing victory in troubled times.

KNOWING WHAT THE WORD SAYS IS NOT ENOUGH

Many make the mistake of just knowing what the Word of God says. They may read their Bible and know what it says, but the Word of God never gets in their heart in abundance. God's Word is not just for reading and knowing, we are supposed to get full of His Word. Many have a head full of knowledge, but their hearts are not full of the Word.

We are not supposed to just know what the Word of God says in our heads. We are supposed to go a step beyond that and have our hearts full of the Word of God. When your heart gets full of the Word, that's when the power of the Word of God will go into action and change your life and even produce victory in troubled times!

YOUR HEART IS A CONTAINER

Our hearts are containers. We must lay hold of that truth. Your heart is a container, and right now as you read this book, it is full of something. In Matthew 12:35, Jesus said, "A good man out of the good treasure of the heart bringeth forth good things: and an evil man out of the evil treasure bringeth forth evil things." The word treasure in that verse means deposit or a place where things are laid up. You can see clearly from this verse that you can deposit things into your heart. This verse tells us we can deposit good things into our hearts, and we can deposit bad things into our hearts.

This truth, that our hearts can be filled, is seen throughout scripture. Let's look at some scriptures of people being full of good things. Romans 15:13 says, "May the God of hope fill you with all joy and peace in believing." Verse 14 says, "That you also are full of goodness, filled with all knowledge, able to admonish one another." Ephesians 3:19 says, "And to know the love of Christ, which passes knowledge, that you might be filled with all the fulness of God." Ephesians 5:18 says, "And be not drunk with wine, wherein excess; but be filled with the Spirit." Acts 5:8 says, "And Stephen, full of faith and power, did great wonders and miracles among the people."

Here are some scriptures of people being full of bad things. Romans 1:29 says, "Being filled with all unrighteousness." Acts 13:45 says, "When the Jews saw the multitudes, they were filled with envy." Lamentations 3:15 says, "He hath filled me with bitterness." Psalm 69:20 says, "I am full of heaviness."

I wanted to reference those verses so that it would become a reality to you that your heart is a container that can be filled. As real as you can fill your gas tank, your heart can be filled. As real as you can fill a pitcher with water, your heart can be filled. As real as you can fill a suitcase with clothes, your heart can be filled.

GOD MADE YOU RESPONSIBLE FOR WHAT FILLS YOUR HEART

We are responsible for what fills our hearts. Colossians 3:16 says, "Let the Word of Christ dwell in you richly." That verse is

140

talking to believers. Therefore, as believers, we are responsible for getting our hearts full of God's Word. God does not do this for us. We cannot pray and ask God to fill our hearts with His Word. Too often, people misuse prayer and try to make God responsible for something He told them to do. It is our responsibility to make sure that our hearts are full of God's Word.

A $300 TANK OF GAS

Your heart is not full of what you want it to be full of, but rather it's full of what you have filled it with. Many want their hearts to be full of God's Word, but they don't fill their hearts with God's Word. The harsh reality is that if you don't put God's Word in your heart, then your heart won't be full of His Word. Anybody that has a bank account can understand the simplicity of that truth. If you don't put money into your account, then there will be no money in your account. You can want your account to be full of money, but your "want" doesn't fill your account with money. Your account is not full of what you want it to be full of. Your account is full of what you have filled it with.

Years ago, I bought a "new" used truck. My old truck took E-85 gasoline. That is an alternative gasoline that you can find at select gas stations, and it usually was a little cheaper in price. When I happened upon a gas station that had that kind of gas, I'd fill my truck up with that. My old truck was the same brand as this new truck we purchased, so I just assumed because it was the same brand that I could put E-85 gasoline in my new truck. One day, shortly after we purchased it, my tank was getting low, so I pulled into a gas station. When I pulled in, I noticed that this particular gas station had E-85 gasoline. I thought to myself, "Oh great. I'll fill up with that and save a few bucks." My tank was really low, so I filled it. I pulled out of the gas station and was driving down the road, and it suddenly dawned on me that I had not checked to see if my new truck took E-85 gasoline. I pulled over to the side of the road, and after a quick google search, I discovered that my new truck did not take E-85 gasoline. I got off of google and called the mechanic. The mechanic told me that I needed to bring it in and get that gas pumped out of there immediately. He proceeded to tell me that it would be around three hundred dollars to do that. Now, at that moment, I did not want my gas tank to be full of E-85 gasoline. I really wanted my tank to be full of regular gasoline. All the "want" in the world wasn't going to change what was in my gas tank. My tank was full of what I filled it with, not what I wanted it to be full of. That was the most expensive tank of gas I have ever purchased.

The same thing is true with your heart. If you are a Christian and you love God, I'm sure you want your heart to be full of God's Word. However, wanting your heart to be full of God's Word does not fill your heart with God's Word. All the "want to" in the world won't fill your heart with God's Word. You can want to have your heart full of God's Word, and intend to fill your heart with His Word, and still not have your heart full of His Word. You have to, consciously and on purpose, fill your heart with what you want it to be full of.

IT'S NOT AUTOMATIC

Being a Christian doesn't ensure that your heart will be full of God's Word. Colossians 3:16 again says, "Let the Word of Christ dwell in you richly." That verse is written to believers. Therefore, it's obvious that just because you are a believer, that does not mean your heart will automatically be full of God's Word. If it was automatic, God wouldn't have to tell us, "Let the Word of Christ dwell in you richly."

A believer can actually have a heart full of the wrong things. Acts 5:3 says, "But Peter said, 'Ananias, why hath Satan filled thine heart to lie to the Holy Ghost.'" Ananias was a believer, yet the enemy had filled his heart with something evil.

If your heart is going to be filled with the Word of God, the necessary deposits must be made. Just because you are a Christian, does not mean your heart is full of the Word of God. Just because you love God, does not mean that your heart is full of the Word of God. Just because you've been born again for twenty years, does not mean that your heart is full of the Word of God. The only people whose hearts are full of the Word of God are the ones who have taken the steps necessary to fill their hearts with it. This does not happen without spiritual effort on our part.

FILL IT UP

Your heart is a lot like the gas tank in your car, in that you fill your tank with gas, you use that supply, and then you have to refill it again. Our hearts are this way. We fill our hearts with the

Word of God, we use that supply, and then we have to refill them again. 2 Corinthians 4:16 says, "Though our outward man perish, yet the inward man is renewed day by day." One definition of the word renewed is to give new strength. Each day your spirit or heart needs a new supply of strength. Why? Because the strength you had yesterday, you used yesterday, and therefore you need to be refilled for today.

In the book of Ephesians, the Apostle Paul is writing to the church of Ephesus. The 19th chapter of Ephesians reveals to us that the church of Ephesus was a Spirit-filled church that spoke in other tongues. In the book of Ephesians, Paul wrote, by the Spirit, to this Spirit-filled church. In chapter 5, verse 17, he said, "Be not drunk with wine, wherein is excess; but be filled with the Spirit." What is he referring to? These believers had already been filled with the Spirit, evidenced by their speaking in other tongues. The International Standard Version of Ephesians 5:18 says, "Keep on being filled with the Spirit." He is revealing to them that even though they were "spirit-filled," they need to keep on being filled. Why would this be so? Because, as believers, in our hearts we use our supply each day, and as a result we need to keep on being filled. We use the supply that is in our hearts for that day, and then we need a fresh filling for tomorrow.

It needs to become a reality to us that being a Christian does not guarantee that our hearts are full of God's Word. You can be a believer whose heart is full of the world's carnal junk. You can be a believer and be completely depleted on the inside where the Word of God is concerned.

If you get depleted on the inside, your chances of experiencing victory in troubled times is nonexistent. If we want to experience victory in troubled times, we must take the time to go to the spiritual filling station and fill our hearts with the Word of God. In a trying time, you will have to fight every day. Every day as you fight to resist the devil and stay in faith, you are consuming your strength inside. If you get depleted inside, you will not possess the strength necessary to endure and experience victory in troubled times.

YOU OPERATE OUT OF YOUR HEART

I mentioned at the beginning of this chapter that keeping your heart full of God's Word is inarguably the most important key to victory in troubled times. The reason that is true is because you operate out of your heart. You function based on what your heart is full of. Proverbs 4:20-23 says, "My son, attend to my words; incline thine ear unto my sayings. Let them not depart from thine eyes; keep them in the midst of thine heart. For they are life unto those that find them, and health to all their flesh. Keep thy heart with all diligence for out of it are the issues of life." The word issues in that verse means outgoings. The outgoings of life come from your heart. Verse 23 in The New International Version says, "Everything you do flows from it [your heart]."

What you do in your life is determined by what has filled your heart. What you believe, what you say and what you do in life comes from what your heart is full of. The choices you make in life are a function of what has filled your heart.

In Matthew 12:35, Jesus said, "A good man out of the good

treasure of the heart bringeth forth good things: and an evil man out of the evil treasure bringeth forth evil things." What you bring forth in life is based on what you have deposited into your heart. This is spiritual law and you cannot change it. The words you bring forth are based on what you have deposited into your heart. The choices you bring forth are based on what you have deposited into your heart. The beliefs you bring forth are based on what you have deposited into your heart. If you want to bring forth words, beliefs and choices that produce victory in troubled times, then you must start by depositing the Word of God into your heart.

As a believer, I have found at times in my life, there is a gap between what I know to do and what I actually do. The Apostle Paul dealt with a similar thing in the seventh chapter of the book of Romans. As believers, we need to be doers of the Word. Knowing what the Word says, but not applying it, will not produce victory in our lives. This gap between what we know to do and what we actually do is created when we have not filled our hearts with the knowledge we have in our heads. You can know something in your head but not be full of it in your heart. When this happens, that gap begins to manifest. The reason why that gap begins to manifest is because we do not operate out of our heads. We do not bring forth out of our heads. Our life is not coming out of our heads. We operate based on what has filled our hearts. Until you get full of what you know, you will not operate according to what you know.

DO YOU HAVE A COLD?

Shortly after I heard the call of God to go into ministry I spent a lot of time in the Word of God. I was working at the golf course at that time and on the days I had to be there by 7:00, I would get up at 5:00 to spend time in the Word. I would take my Bible with me to work and study if there was downtime. I was listening to preaching and teaching a lot. Needless to say, my heart was full of the Word of God.

One day, a customer asked me to join him for nine holes after I got off work and I accepted. This man was a customer at the golf course, and I did not know him very well. We had spoken a few times, but these were just the common pleasantries that take place between a customer and an employee.

I got off work, clocked out, threw my bag on the back of the golf cart and jumped in with him. The skies were gray, and it was a cool, wet day. He drove the golf cart over to the first tee, and as he stopped the cart I sneezed. On that particular day, I happened to be dealing with some cold symptoms. Along with the sneeze, I had a congested nose. Based on the way I was talking and the sneeze that just occurred, he said, "Do you have a cold?" This would be a very normal question to ask someone who was displaying the symptoms that I was.

Well, the Lord had been teaching me about faith in God and the power of my words. I had been feeding on that for months, so my heart was full of it. When he asked me that question, before I could think, I said, "No," in response to his question. It felt like it just slipped out of my mouth. I knew this man probably had never heard about faith in God and the power of our words, so I never would have answered him like that intentionally. I would have found a way to answer the question in a way that he understood. I do not think it does any good for Christians to act unnecessarily strange around people who do not understand what we are doing. Well, after that word "no" slipped out of my mouth, it was awkwardly silent for about 15 seconds. Then we teed it up and got on with our round of golf.

I told you that story to demonstrate to you that what you do in life is determined by what your heart is full of. That word, "no," slipped out of my mouth because my heart was full of what the Word of God said about faith, about the power of my words and about healing. I was operating based on what I had filled my heart with.

WHY DID I DO THAT?

Effectively, we are at the mercy of whatever has filled our hearts. To illustrate this, I want to look at a lengthy passage of scripture in Luke 8:27-35. It says,

There met him [Jesus] out of the city a certain man, which had devils long time, and ware no clothes, neither abode in any house, but in the tombs. 29For he had commanded the unclean spirit to come out of the man. For oftentimes it had caught him: and he was kept bound with chains and in fetters; and he brake the bands, and was driven of the devil into the wilderness. 30And Jesus asked him, saying, "What is thy name?" And he said, "Legion": because many devils were entered into him. 31And they besought him that he would not command them to go out into the deep. 32And there was there an herd of many swine feeding on the mountain: and they besought him that he would suffer them to enter into them. And he suffered them. 33Then went the devils out of the man, and entered into the swine: and the herd ran violently down a steep place into the lake, and were choked. 35Then they went out to see what was done; and came to Jesus, and found the man, out of whom the devils were departed, sitting at the feet of Jesus, clothed, and in his right mind: and they were afraid.

As long as this man was full of devils, he was at the mercy of those devils. This is why he did not wear clothes. This is why he lived in the tombs. This man was driven by the devil into the wilderness because we are at the mercy of whatever has filled our hearts.

After Jesus commanded the devils to come out of the man, he was no longer naked and living in the tombs, but sitting at the feet of Jesus, clothed and in his right mind. Why? Because once he was no longer full of devils, he was no longer at the mercy of those devils. In fact, you'll notice that those devils entered into a herd of pigs, and the pigs ran off of a cliff. Why didn't the pigs run off the cliff the day before? Because they were not full of devils the day before. Once they were full of devils, they were at the mercy of what had filled them.

You cannot be full of something and operate in opposition to it. You cannot function in opposition to what has filled your heart. In Matthew 12:33-35, Jesus said,

Either make the tree good and his fruit good; or else make the tree corrupt and his fruit corrupt: for the tree is known by his fruit. O generation of vipers, how can you, being evil speak good things? For out of the abundance of the heart the mouth speaks. A good man out of the good treasure (deposit) of the heart brings forth good things; and an evil man out of the evil treasure brings forth evil things.

A corrupt tree cannot bring forth good fruit because inside it is full of corruption. A good tree cannot bring forth corrupt fruit because inside it is full of goodness. These people that Jesus was speaking to, in Matthew 12, were full of evil; being full of evil, they could not bring forth good words. An evil man who makes evil deposits into his heart cannot bring forth good things. A good man who makes good deposits into his heart cannot bring forth evil things. You cannot be full of something and operate in opposition to it.

Have you ever said something that you wished you wouldn't have said? Why did you say it? Because you are at the mercy of what has filled your heart. Have you ever done something that after the fact you wished you had not done? Why did you do it? Because you are at the mercy of what has filled your heart.

Your heart is a container, and you operate out of what is in that container. This is spiritual law and you can't change it. You function based on what your heart is full of. Whatever your heart is full of is what you will bring forth in your life.

THE FULL HEART & VICTORY IN TROUBLED TIMES

What does having your heart full of God's Word have to do with experiencing victory in troubled times? Everything.

If you want to experience victory in troubled times, then you have to operate a certain way in the midst of those troubled times. Your victory in troubled times is not all up to God. Let me remind you of what Jesus said to Jairus in Luke 8 after Jairus had gotten a report that his daughter was dead. In verse 50, Jesus said, "Fear not, believe only and she shall be made whole." You can see from Jesus' words that what Jairus does in this troubled time has everything to do with the outcome that he will experience. Jesus did not say, "Jairus, it does not matter what you do. It is the predetermined will of God for your daughter to live, so it is going to happen." If Jairus wants to win, he must operate a certain way. He must stay in faith and stay out of fear.

In Mark 9, there was a man who brought his son to Jesus. His son was possessed with a devil, and he wanted Jesus to help his son. In verse 22, he said to Jesus, "If you can do anything, have compassion on us and help us." He was trying to put all the responsibility for his son being delivered in Jesus' lap. Jesus said to him in verse 23, "If you can believe, all things are possible to him that believes." Jesus was revealing to this man that he had a part to play in seeing his son delivered. If this man wants to enjoy victory in this troubled time, then he has to operate a certain way. He is to operate by faith in the midst of this troubled time if he wants to experience victory.

What we do in the midst of a trying time is a major component in us experiencing victory in the trying time. People like to pretend that whether or not they experience victory in troubled times is all up to God, but that simply is not true. We have a part to play when it comes to experiencing victory in troubled times. The good news is that God will show us what our part is, give us grace to do our part and correct us if we are letting our part slip a little bit. We are not alone. God will help us. Our victory is not all up to us. We have a part and God has a part. If we want to experience victory in troubled times, then we must do our part.

WHAT IT TAKES TO WIN

To experience victory in troubled times there are certain things we must do. Over the next few pages, I want to give you a few principles of victory. These are basic things we must do if we want to prevail over our adversary. This is not an exhaustive list of the principles of victory, but a few major ones.

The first principle of victory is that we must stay in faith. 1 John 5:4 says, "For whatsoever is born of God overcomes the world: and this is the victory that overcomes the world even our faith." Having faith in God, living by faith, walking by faith: this is how we overcome obstacles in life. Hebrews 11:32–34 says,

And what shall I more say? for the time would fail me to tell of Gedeon, and of Barak, and of Samson, and of Jephthae; of David also, and Samuel, and of the prophets: Who through faith subdued kingdoms, wrought righteousness, obtained promises, stopped the mouths of lions. Quenched the violence of fire, escaped the edge of the sword, out of weakness were made strong, waxed valiant in fight, turned to flight the armies of the aliens.

These people overcome obstacles in their lives through faith in God. They operated by faith right in the middle of troubled times, and faith in God produced victory in their lives. You and I will not experience victory in troubled times if we do not stay in faith.

The second principle of victory is that we must hold fast to the Word of God. We have to continue to believe the Word and speak the Word in spite of what we see and feel. In Mark 4:15, Jesus said, "Satan comes immediately, and takes away the Word that was sown in their hearts." The enemy targets the Word of God in our lives, and if we let go of God's Word and stop believing it and stop speaking it, then we will not experience victory in troubled times. God revealed to us in Joshua 1:8 that His Word is a central component in our success. In Joshua 1:8, God said, "This book of the law shall not depart out of your mouth; but you shall meditate therein day and night, that you may observe to do according to all that is written therein: for then you shall make your way prosperous, and then you shall have good success."

The third principle of victory is that we have to persevere in the face of adversity. If you get weak and quit, you will not win. Galatians 6:9 says, "Let us not be weary in well doing: for in due season we will reap, if we faint not." In Luke 8, Jesus was talking about sowing the seed of God's Word and seeing it produce. In verse 15, he said, "But that on the good ground are they, which in an honest and good heart, having heard the Word, keep it, and bring forth fruit with patience." The word patience in that verse means constancy or perseverance. You have to be constant and persevere if you want to see God's Word produce victory in troubled times. Hebrews 6:12 confirms this by saying, "That you be not slothful, but followers of them who through faith and patience inherit the promises." Victory in troubled times is a promise from God, but you will not enjoy it without patience and perseverance. So many people never enjoy victory because they get weak and quit. Proverbs 24:10 says, "If you faint in the day of adversity, thy strength is small."

These principles of victory are just a few ways that we have to function in the midst of a trying time if we want to experience victory.

THE IMPORTANCE OF FILLING YOUR HEART

This next statement might be the most important thing you'll read in this book: It is impossible for you to operate — the way you need to operate — and to experience victory in troubled times if your heart is not full of the Word of God. Go back and read that again. Friend, you operate out of your heart. If your heart is not full of the Word, you will not be able to operate by faith. If your heart is not full of the Word, you will not be able to hold fast to the Word in spite of what you see and feel. If your heart is not full of the Word, you will not be able to persevere in the face of adversity. Why? Because you operate out of your heart.

One of the biggest problems people have in experiencing victory in troubled times is that they do not fill their hearts in a way that enables them to operate at peak capacity — in a way that sets them up to experience victory in troubled times. If your heart is depleted where the Word is concerned, you don't stand a chance in a troubled time because you operate out of that container. If your heart is not full of the Word, you cannot operate according to the Word. If your heart is not full of the Word, you can't operate by faith. If your heart is not full of the Word, you won't decree the Word in the face of negative

154

circumstances. If your heart is not full of the Word, you'll get weak inside and won't be able to persevere in the face of adversity. You will only operate the way you need to when your heart is full of the Word.

One of the most important things you can do to experience victory in troubled times is to get your heart full of God's Word and keep your heart full of God's Word. I cannot overstate the importance of what I just said to you. Filling your heart with God's word and keeping it full will keep your faith high. This will keep your strength high. It will enable you to hold fast to God's Word and persevere in the face of adversity. It will enable you to believe what God says and say what He says right in the face of negative circumstances and evil reports. You cannot stop a person who has filled their heart with God's Word. They are warriors! They won't quit! They are the fighters who refuse to lose! They are the champions who will enjoy victory! They will believe what God says no matter how bad it looks! They will say what God says in the face of evil reports! When it is dark and all hope of victory seems lost, from the midst of that darkness, faith will come roaring out of their hearts! They thrive in times of pressure! They persevere in the face of adversity! They do not get weak! They do not retreat! They do not relent! Why is this so? Because they are operating out of their hearts, and their hearts are full of God's Word!

HOW TO FILL YOUR HEART WITH GOD'S WORD

Learning how to fill your heart with God's Word is one of the most important things you can learn in your life. That is not hyperbole. Understanding how to take God's Word from the written page and fill your heart with it is absolutely vital information that every believer must have.

In understanding how to fill your heart with God's Word, we must first gain concept of how things get into our hearts. In Matthew 6:22-23, Jesus said, "The light of the body is the eye: if therefore thine eye be single, thy whole body shall be full of light. But if thine eye be evil, thy whole body shall be full of darkness."

Let's look at this phrase, "the light of the body." The word body in this verse is referring to your being, not just your physical body. This verse could read as, "The light of the being is the eye." The word light in this verse is not used the way we use light in our modern English language. When we hear the word light, we think about something that emanates light, like the sun or a light bulb. In this verse, the word light means a place that allows light to enter or a place where light gets in. For example, you could say the light of the house is the windows. The window is not the light itself, but it's the place where light enters. When Jesus said the light of the body is the eye, he was saying the entryway into your being is the eye. The eye is the place where things get into your being. The word eye in this verse refers to the eyes of the mind. Therefore, to say that the light of the body is the eye, is to say that the entryway into your being is the mind.

Your mind is the entryway into your heart. Anything that goes into the mind will get into your heart. If light comes through your windows, light gets in the house. If darkness comes through your windows, darkness gets in the house. Anything that comes through your mind gets into your heart.

What you do with your mind has everything to do with what fills your heart. What you look at, think on and focus on is what you will get full of. The focus determines the fill. Jesus said in Matthew 6:22-23, "If your eye be single, your whole body will be full of light. But if your eye be evil, thy whole body shall be full of darkness." He is making the connection between what you focus on and what you are full of.

To get our hearts full of God's Word, we must purposefully focus on it, feed on it and think about it. As we do this, God's Word will go through our minds and begin to fill our hearts. God revealed this truth to us in Deuteronomy 11:18-20 (The Message Bible). It says,

Place these words on your hearts. Get them deep inside you. Tie them on your hands and foreheads as a reminder. Teach them to your children. Talk about them wherever you are, sitting at home or walking in the street; talk about them from the time you get up in the morning until you fall into bed at night. Inscribe them on the doorposts and gates of your cities.

God started off by telling them to put His Words in their hearts, and then He told them how to do it. The way to get the Word of God into your heart is to keep it in front of you all the time. Looking at His Word, studying His Word, reading His Word, talking about His Word and meditating upon His Word is how you get full of it. That's why God told His people in Deuteronomy to talk about the Word all the time, write it on the doorposts of their houses and tie it upon their hands and foreheads. What was God telling them? Keep it in front of you and it will get in you!

You cannot get full of what you don't focus on, feed on, listen to, think about and look at. That is a spiritual law. Lamentations 3:51 says, "My eyes [mental faculties]) affect my heart." The writer is telling us that what he was looking at and thinking on, affected him on the inside. The only way to get your heart full of God's Word is to feed on it.

IN TROUBLED TIMES
KEEP THE WORD GOING IN

It is critically important in troubled times to keep feeding the Word of God into your heart. Being in ministry for close to 20 years now, I have seen people who decide to stop going to church because they are going through a hard time. The reality is, that is the exact opposite of what they should do. They need to get their heart full of the Word of God, and one of the best ways you can do that is to listen to His Word preached. In times of trouble, you need your heart to be full of God's Word, and the only way to get your heart full of God's Word is to feed on it.

In times of pressure, you need to closely monitor the level of God's Word you have in your heart, and make sure to keep your heart full. Why? Because you operate out of your heart. Proverbs 4:23 says, "For out of it [the heart] are the issues of life." The Message Bible says, "That's where life starts." The Evangelical Heritage Version says, "Your life flows from it." What your heart is full of affects how you operate, and the way you operate affects whether or not you enjoy victory or experience defeat. What your heart is full of affects what you believe, what you say, what you do and the choices you make, and those things affect what you experience in your life. If your heart begins to get low where the Word of God is concerned, you won't be able to operate the way you need to in order to experience victory in troubled times.

Therefore, it is vitally important to keep the Word of God going in you when you are in the middle of troubled times. You need to be listening to good teaching and preaching. You need to be speaking the Word of God, concerning your situation. You need to be meditating the Word of God, concerning your situation. You can even put scriptures up all around your house, concerning your situation. All this is necessary if your heart is going to get full and stay full of God's Word. You have to keep feeding the Word into you no matter how great the pressure gets. No matter how hopeless your situation seems, you have to make it a priority to keep your heart full of the Word of God. If you get depleted on the inside, victory becomes an impossibility. However, if you get full of the Word of God and stay full of the Word of God, all of hell can't stop you from experiencing victory in troubled times!

SCRIPTURES IN THE TOILET

Bill Winston, a pastor in Chicago, Illinois, once told a story about his wife when she was believing for a job. I believe things were tight for them financially at the time, so his wife was believing for a job. He said she kept the Word of God in front of her all the time. One way she did that was by putting scriptures up all over the house. He said you would walk to the refrigerator, and on it there would be a scripture. He said you would go to the cabinet, and on it there would be a scripture. He said you would go to the bathroom, and on the mirror, there would be a scripture. He then laughed and jokingly said, you lifted the toilet seat up, and there would be a scripture. The point he was making is that she kept her heart full of the Word where that job was concerned.

One day she got a call from the employment office. They told her they found her resume in the bottom of a desk drawer. They told her that they thought they had a job for her with a company that was perfect for her. She set up an interview with that company, and they offered her a job.

Now, she had a list of all the things she wanted in that job. She wanted it to be in computers and it was. She wanted it to pay a certain amount, and they offered her $10,000 more than that. She wanted them to get her a company car, and they told her she could go to the dealership and pick out a car. It was the supernatural favor of God that produced that job in her life.

One of the things that enabled her to stay in faith and persevere when it looked like she would never get a job is that she kept her heart full of God's Word by keeping it in front of her all the time.

As we close out this chapter, ask yourself, "What steps am I going to take to make sure that my heart gets full and stays full of the Word of God?" The more troubling your situation is, the more radical you will have to be where this is concerned. You may need to turn the TV off. You may need to stay off social media. Replace that with time spent in the Word of God. Do whatever is necessary to get your heart full of God's Word because with a heart full of God's Word you are positioned to experience victory in troubled times. When your heart is full of God's Word, all of hell cannot keep you from enjoying the victory that God wants for you!

CHAPTER 7

PUT THE PRINCIPLES INTO PRACTICE

It thrills The Father to see His children walking in victory. Psalm 35:27 says, "Let them shout for joy, and be glad, that favor my righteous cause: yea, let them say continually, Let the Lord be magnified, which hath pleasure in the prosperity of his servant." One definition of the word, "prosperity" in this verse means to do well. God gets great pleasure in His people doing well and walking in victory.

It is the desire of my heart to see you experience victory in troubled times. I want to see you come out of the low place and into a place of triumph. I want to see you do well in your life. It brings great joy to my heart to see God's people walk in victory.

The truth is, there is no "formula" that will produce victory in your life. That is to say, "You do one, two and three and you will experience victory." Spiritual battles are not linear. There are ups and downs, hills and valleys, highs and lows. Spiritual battles don't always play out the way you expect. Things can happen in spiritual battles that you don't see coming. Every spiritual battle you face in life is different. Each one will demand different things for you to experience victory.

Although there is no formula that will produce victory in your life, there are principles of victory that work! There are certain things that we can do in every battle that will position us to experience victory in our lives. God gave us principles of victory in His Word. I have laid out five of these truths in this book. The great thing about these precepts is that they will travel. You can take these principles of victory into any battle you are facing and, if you will apply them, they will position you to experience victory in your life.

These principles of victory will only work for you, if you practice them. This is true in many areas of life. For example, let's look at weight loss. There are principles that govern weight loss. These are things a person must do if they desire to lose weight. You can know the principles of weight loss, read books about the principles of weight loss, study the principles of weight loss, but until you put those principles into practice you will never lose weight. Just knowing the principles of victory will not produce victory in your life. If you want to experience victory in troubled times, you must apply the things you have learned in this book.

One major thing that will help you put these principles of victory into practice is to keep them in front of you. We find this in James 1:22-25. It says, "But be ye doers of the word, and not hearers only, deceiving your own selves. 23 For if any be a hearer of the word, and not a doer, he is like unto a man beholding his natural face in a glass: 24 For he beholds himself, and goeth his way, and straightway forgetteth what manner of man he was. 25 But whoso looketh into the perfect law of liberty, and continueth therein, he being not a forgetful hearer, but a doer of the work, this man shall be blessed in his deed." In these verses we find two men. One man was a doer of the Word and the other man was not. The only difference between them was that one kept the Word in front of him and the other did not. If you don't keep these principles of victory in front of you, you will not be a doer of them.

It is my heart's desire to conclude this book in such a way that you are left feeling inspired. However, inspiration built on a false reality will not lead to victory in your life. Therefore, I am going to give it to you straight, and hope that you are inspired by it.

There will be two types of people that read this book. One will read this book and maybe even enjoy it, but just set it on the shelf and apply little or nothing they read. Those people will not experience victory in troubled times. They will struggle. Their lives will not change. They will live under the enemy's thumb. All they will be left with is the haunting reality that they could have experienced victory in their life had they been willing to do what they learned.

Others will read this book and determine in their heart to do what they learned. They will keep the principles of victory in front of them. They will put the principles of victory into practice. They will stick with it when it gets tough. When they are tired, they won't quit. When they are under attack, they won't give in. When all hell is breaking loose, when all hope seems gone, when the majority of believers on the planet would tuck tail and run, they won't draw back, but instead they will push back against the enemy and everything he's trying to do in their lives. These are the ones who will experience victory in troubled times.

Let's go to work!

ABOUT THE AUTHOR

Matthew Allaria is the founder of Matthew Allaria Ministries and the pastor of Northsmoke Church in Collinsville, Illinois.

Matthew is anointed to teach people the Word Of God. His heart is to train people up to a high place in faith and in the Word Of God. He has a great passion for God's Word and a strong desire to see people experience God's best in their lives.

In the early morning hours of November 7, 2003, Matthew received the call to the ministry. On April 1, 2004, he received his first invitation to preach at a church in Southern Illinois. In January 2005, Matthew founded Matthew Allaria Ministries and began hosting weekly services and conferences. On March 14, 2007, he went into full-time ministry. Matthew graduated from Jerry Savelle Ministries School Of Ministry in April 2007. In January 2019 Matthew launched The Faith For Life Broadcast which airs every week Monday through Friday on YouTube. In January of

2020, Matthew and his wife Amber launched Northsmoke Church. Matthew has taught over 100 series, wrote articles, produced study notes and created declarations of faith all in his desire to see believers grow spiritually and experience victory in their lives.

Matthew currently resides in Edwardsville, IL with his wife Amber and two daughters Grace and Faith.

Made in USA - Kendallville, IN
39882_9781954966178
07.07.2022 1405